WILD
swimming
SYDNEY

250 best rock pools,
beaches, rivers and waterholes

Sally Tertini & Steve Pollard

WILD
swimming
SYDNEY

WILD THINGS PUBLISHING

Contents

Regional Overview

Sydney is the Harbour City and it's difficult to imagine somewhere offering more watery possibilities. For the wild swimmer, it really has it all!

We exalt the famed beaches that string together like a tantalising necklace up and down our coastline, but most of us rarely venture farther than our favourite local haunt. It's so easy to jet across the world and explore distant lands that we often forget to spend time discovering what's in our own backyard!

If you don't mind swimming in waves, then all you need to do is head east and charge in. If, however, you prefer a bit of diversity, and like the idea of swimming unhindered by choppy surf, then this book is for you!

Fancy an invigorating dip beneath the thundering charge of a towering waterfall? Or wildly leaping from a rock ledge into crystalline water? How about discovering you have a hidden cove all to yourself, and enjoying the liberating sensation of saltwater against your bare skin?

Whether you just like to paddle about on a hot day, or enjoy the challenge of a long explorative swim; whether you love the thrill of hurling yourself off a rope swing, or leisurely floating downstream, Wild Swimming Sydney will guide you to tucked-away gems, as well as making you see the Sydney you already know in a whole new light!

So why not jump in and reinvigorate the way you see this great city?

Acknowledgement of Country

The colonization of Australia had a far reaching and devastating impact on its indigenous people. Australia was, of course, not terra nullius - the area covered in this book alone being home to many Aboriginal tribal groups.

We would like to pay respect to these traditional owners of the land, and acknowledge that it is within their ancestral lands we swim. As we share our own knowledge and passion for wild swimming in Sydney, may we also pay respect to the knowledge embedded forever within the Aboriginal Custodianship of Country.

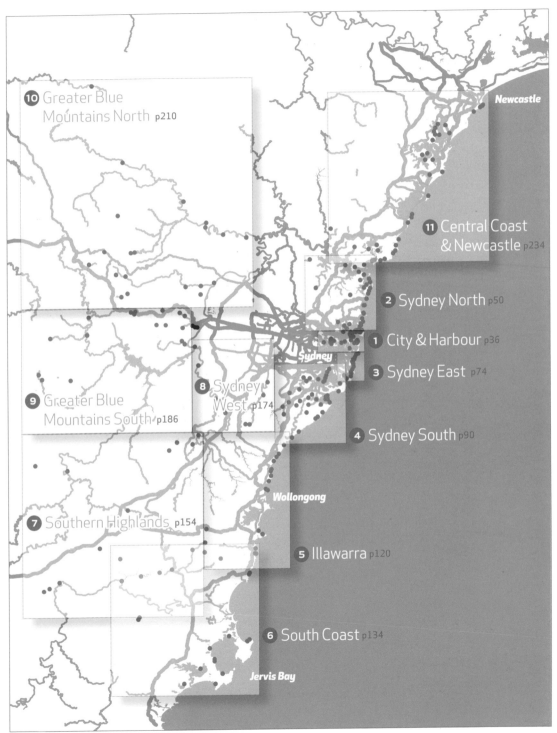

10 Greater Blue Mountains North *p210*

Newcastle

11 Central Coast & Newcastle *p234*

2 Sydney North *p50*

1 City & Harbour *p36*

Sydney

3 Sydney East *p74*

8 Sydney West *p174*

9 Greater Blue Mountains South *p186*

4 Sydney South *p90*

Wollongong

7 Southern Highlands *p154*

5 Illawarra *p120*

6 South Coast *p134*

Jervis Bay

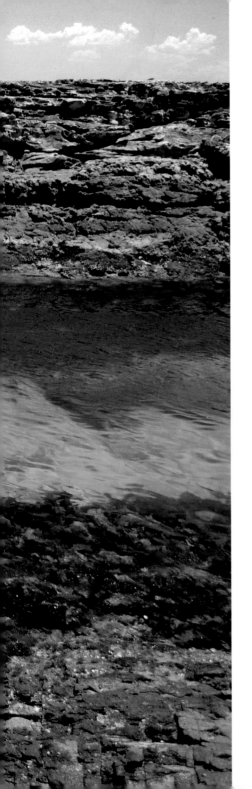

Introduction

WHAT IS WILD SWIMMING?

To be clear, no-one's trying to reinvent the wheel here – wild swimming is just, well, swimming! And while you've probably been doing it for years, a few key points differentiate the wild swimmer from your garden-variety swim enthusiast.

Put simply, wild swimming is swimming for pleasure in natural waters. It's swimming with no particular goal in mind, other than to experience the sheer joy that immersion brings. Wild swimming also allows us to reconnect with the natural world – something that has become rare in our modern, urban lives. It shows us that nature is, in fact, not remote, but still abundant and readily accessible.

The 'wild' part connotes swimming in natural waters. It's not restricted to far-flung and pristine wilderness areas, but creeks, rivers, waterholes, lakes, dams, lagoons, beaches, bogey holes and ocean baths everywhere. The 'swimming' component is also fairly open to interpretation; you can plunge, dip, wade, paddle, float, swim, bob, frolic and wallow.

Australians love the water – most of us live on the fringe of the biggest island on the planet. Many of our national heroes are swimmers, adored for the grit and physical prowess which enables them to endure gruelling sea crossings, or swim lap after lap with uniform precision. Wild swimming, however, is not competitive – nor is it about prevailing over the elements. Instead, it's about becoming a part of the natural world around us. There's also something very democratic about being stripped down to our cossies, with little to differentiate us.

While you still get some of the benefits associated with physical activity, fun is emphasised over fitness. Wild swimming couldn't give a toss about technique or personal bests. Whether you sit in a frothy natural jacuzzi for five minutes, or follow a curving river downstream for 2km, what matters is your experience.

"You see and experience things when you're swimming in a way that is completely different from any other. You are in nature, part and parcel of it, in a far more complete and intense way than on dry land, and your sense of the present is overwhelming."

Roger Deakin

Stepping away from the familiar and rediscovering wild places carries a deep appeal. Wild swimming lets us embrace the freedom of the great outdoors unencumbered by the daily constraints of urban life. And even if only for a short time, it connects us with something ancient and uncomplicated. When you get down to it, wild swimming is more a state of mind than a sport!

THE BENEFITS OF WILDNESS AND SWIMMING

The bush looms large in the global view of Australia, but more importantly it's a big part of our own mythology. Even though most of us are urban dwellers these days, we can't shake the feeling that it's still a part of who we are.

For a lot of us there's an inkling that for all the advances in our modern, hyper-connected lives, something has also been lost. In large measure, we have become insulated and disconnected from the natural world – so much of our lives are now spent inside staring at screens. Many of us are trapped on the hamster wheel of modern life and, as well as leaving us exhausted, it makes us lose sight of our own wild and unbridled selves. Happily, though, we can shake off the stresses of our lives, even for a little while, and get back to basics. Wildness is the antidote to modern living.

Wild swimming literally immerses us in nature, and gives us access to a whole new world. Surrounded by all that, we seem "to shrink and shrink," as Annette Kellerman put it. With that vague possibility of becoming lost amid the vastness, we get a refreshing sense of perspective. Allowing ourselves to be dwarfed by the enormity and becoming part of our environment, we can experience a reassuring sense of inter-connectedness. What's more, it's humbling to be faced with something bigger than ourselves and so much more enduring than anything built by humans.

The wilds represent an untamed domain and, even in man-made ocean baths there's always the wildcard of nature. We may understand the principals, but we're never in charge. This vulnerability brings us right into the moment, and gives us an invigorating dose of aliveness.

No two wild swim spots are the same, and even one location can change completely from one day to the next. We're forced to engage

with the natural world – buffeted by the swell of the ocean and carried by the current of a river. You're suddenly on the same level as the natural world, which is disarming.

Backyard pools remain the domain of the privileged, and municipal pools have opening hours, rules and entry fees. Swimming in a chlorinated pool will always be swimming in a box. There's no sense of exploration or discovery. Wild swimming gets you away from all of that – it's swimming on your own terms with no finite borders. Its boundless nature not only invites exploration, but with no set edges, the distinction between us and the world around us blurs. In a chlorinated pool we are separated from the feeling of sand underfoot, the fizzing pop of surging waves and the fragrant scent of eucalypt leaves. Rivers, beaches and rock pools are living, breathing ecosystems, with much more to see and feel than tiled walls and lane markers.

Intuitively, we feel that being in nature is good for us – that it somehow recharges the batteries – but there is also some incredible scientific research being done which is revealing just how deep this goes.

Just being in nature makes us feel good, with one study showing that a mere 20 minutes is enough to improve feelings of self-esteem, to lower blood pressure and reduce tension, anger and depression.

What's more, other studies have shown that exercising outside has more benefits than exercising indoors.

Just being near running water can have a calming effect. The movement of water releases negative ions into the air, which help balance out levels of seratonin, resulting in you feeling happier and more relaxed.

There's also something meditative about the rhythmical motion of gliding through water as you swim. The repetitive movements activate your parasympathetic nervous system and move you into a place of relaxation.

Evidence also shows that water temperature has a part to play, with studies suggesting that cold-water swimming can help everything from arthritic pain to depression. Swimming in cold water releases a flood of adrenaline, cortisol and endorphins – a heady cocktail leading to the high that swimmers often experience.

Of course, there's also the usual benefits from physical exercise, and unlike almost all other physical activities, you can swim for life. When you swim your body only bears 10 per cent of its own weight, and this weightlessness is transforming. So, not only will wild swimming make you feel great, it'll probably do you some good too!

HISTORY OF WILD SWIMMING IN SYDNEY

From its first swimmers – the region's Aboriginals – people have been swimming in Sydney for thousands of years.

Local Aboriginals are described in early European accounts as being strong and competent swimmers. They swam both for pleasure and to fish, but also for spiritual reasons. Rivers and waterholes are sacred places in Aboriginal culture. They were created during the Dreamtime by ancestor spirits, who are said to still inhabit them. It was believed that these ancestor spirits imparted particular qualities to the swimmer, such as strength and intelligence. Because of this cultural importance, waterholes were usually the first places to be named, with the surrounding areas then being named after them.

When Europeans began to arrive in Sydney in the late 1700s, they bought with them the culture of the day. Sea-bathing at the time was considered to be therapeutic to both body and mind, and a necessary antidote to the impact of urban life on cleanliness and morality. Sydney's hot climate and vast coastline made it ideally suited to the pastime, and the city's gentry took up sea-bathing with gusto.

By the mid-1800s, swimming from the beach in daylight had been made illegal in the name of decency, and ocean and harbour baths began to spring up across the city. Many new baths were sited at places historically used by Aboriginals.

Following both Aboriginal and contemporary English practices – bathing was segregated, and many suburbs had both men's and women's baths. Men generally swam naked, while women wore bulky swimming dresses and pantaloons. The cost of bathing costumes meant that swimming for women remained a pursuit for the middle class. One of the first baths to allow mixed bathing was Wylie's in Coogee.

"I never concern myself about the good or harm swimming does me, or whether it will lengthen or shorten my life. It has enabled me to live more fully and happily. And that in itself is enough."

Jack Overhill

In 1902, the laws banning daylight bathing were finally challenged. A maverick newspaper editor, William Gocher, had the spunk to announce his intention to swim at Manly Beach at noon one Sunday. An overwhelming public outcry followed Gocher's arrest, and the laws were eased to again allow daylight bathing. Ocean swimming surged in popularity.

Soon after, on February 21st 1907, the worldwide Surf Life Saving movement was born at Bondi Beach. Lifeguards also started appearing at popular riverside swimming spots such as the Cooks River. It seems almost inconceivable that the Cooks – now the sewer of the Inner West, was, until recently, a popular swimming spot. Even Australian movie star and swim icon, Annette Kellerman, regularly swam in these river baths. At the time you could also find dozens of men and boys frolicking naked in the river. In 1908 the Nepean River was dammed at Camden, creating a large area of deep water, ideal for swimming. Over in Manly, Mermaids Pool was so named for the hordes of girls who would swim naked in its sparkling water in the 1930s, and had an even longer history of use by Aboriginals.

A gradual shift away from swimming in natural waters started in 1933, with the appearance of Sydney's first chlorinated Olympic swimming pools – built in response to new international rules regulating competitive swimming. Following World War II, Australia experienced a golden era in competitive swimming, which not only helped galvanise a national identity separate from Britain, but also saw public interest in these standardised pools grow. Chlorinated pools became a symbol of modernity, and were soon seen as an essential public amenity. In the 1950s Camden Council responded to a call to open a chlorinated pool by saying that the Nepean River had been good enough for generations of swimmers before, so why build a pool? Greater Sydney, however, was experiencing a population explosion, and this growth, coupled with poor management, lead to a noticeable deterioration in the quality of both fresh and saltwater. By 1964, pollution in the Nepean River had become so bad that a municipal pool was finally opened. Rivers across the city faced similar problems, and for swimmers, the new council-run chlorinated pools became even more appealing.

"However the world seemed
before a wild swim, it always looks
fantastic afterwards."

Daniel Start

Come the 1970s, growing public awareness over environmental issues, and the popularisation of surf culture, led to a demand for cleaner beaches. Local governments finally pledged to stop discharging raw effluent in the early 1980s, and replacement deep-water ocean outfalls were constructed. At the same time there was a campaign to raise public awareness of stormwater run-off pollution. Ocean water quality improved and Sydney-siders returned in droves to swim at our beaches and baths.

Widespread interest in the water quality of Sydney's rivers has occurred more recently. It's sadly now more common to see abandoned shopping trolleys in the waters of evocatively named places such as Blue Hole and Fishponds than the swimmers that once filled them. Even in the Blue Mountains, many once-deep pools have become silted up from building works. However, many of our fresh waterways are now monitored for pollution by the admirable Streamwatch program. Grassroots rehabilitation campaigns have also sprung up across Sydney, and local governments are slowly acknowledging residents' desire to see their rivers thriving again. Initiatives are now under-way along the Cooks, Georges and Parramatta rivers to make them clean enough for swimming once more!

Swim Safari

It's easy to go on a swim safari

1. **Don't rush:** really savour each wild swim location you visit.

2. **Make the journey part of the fun:** stop off on the way!

3. **Travel slow:** try leaving the car at home and catching public transport or cycling.

4. **Get local:** fuel up post-swim by trying out local eateries or tucking into regional delicacies.

5. **Keep off the beaten track:** explore back-roads, and steer clear of tourist attractions.

6. **Stay a while:** travel by campervan, stay in a B&B, or camp.

It's not just surfers who can go on safari! Dose up on wild swimming and go on a swim safari! Safari comes from the Arabic word "safar" – meaning to take a journey or trip – and what could be better than dedicating some time to exploring a new place, by literally immersing yourself in the environment? Wild swimming leaves you feeling buoyant, but the full tonic comes when you stay a while.

Going on a swim safari emboldens us, visitors and locals alike, to experience a place rather than just look at it. It encourages us to reconsider what we thought we already knew, and to hook in with all our senses!

Every place has its own unique kind of magic, but it's generally not something that reveals itself readily. Swim safariing helps you unlock the secrets of a place by enabling you to become a part of it. Your swim safari can be a one-day adventure or a week-long odyssey: plan an itinerary with great detail, or see where the current takes you.

Use the Best Places For index and the region maps to help you plan your swim safari. Select a fantastic swim spot as your end destination, then add some stop-off swims for the trip there and back. You can stay in the city and have an urban swim safari, or head out into the bush.

Camping is a great way to prolong your stay, and it's also a terrific accompaniment to wild swimming. Many locations in this book also offer camping options, running the full gamut from glamping grounds with all amenities to remote bush campsites with none. Camping lets you unplug from the modern world – with time, all the to-do lists zipping through your mind slip away, and you fall into step with the natural rhythms around you.

With life stripped back to basics, a new sense of perspective can emerge. The usual modern markers of happiness go out the window – in beautiful surrounds, a cosy bed, a full belly and good company are more than enough! What's more, with this new perspective, a more intrinsic sense of self can surface – one that is often quite different to that of your everyday life.

Campfires are an integral part of the camping experience – building, tending and watching a fire all speak to primal parts of our being, and stir something deep within. Children and adults alike are at once calmed and enlivened by mesmeric flames, and cooking on a fire gives a real sense of self-sufficiency.

Whichever kind of swim safari you choose, you'll have the sense of being a pilgrim exploring the city's riches. And as you experience a place over time, its beauty tends to increase, and your connection to it becomes stronger. So that as you get to know Sydney in intimate detail, its places will become *your* places.

What to take on bushwalks

1. Food and water – you should figure on one litre of water per person. You can also bring purification tablets, which let you top up your bottle straight from the river.

2. A travel towel that's quick-drying and compact.

3. Shoes with good grip – these make slips and falls less likely.

4. A first-aid kit.

5. Warm clothes – even in summer.

6. Maps – absolutely essential in some cases. They can help get you out of the bush if you lose your way.

7. Matches – as a precaution should you become lost.

8. A compass.

9. A GPS device – allows you to track time and distance, which is helpful when following directions.

10. A Personal Locator Beacon (PLB) – these devices are able to send out a locatable stress signal if you get into trouble. Free PLBs are available for loan in the Blue Mountains from the NPWS Office, Govetts Leap Rd, Blackheath, or after hours from the Police Stations in Katoomba or Springwood.

See the annex for more information on safety and access.

Other useful info

Temperature and rainfall

Check the latest temperature and rainfall forecasts for different areas around Sydney: www.bom.gov.au/nsw/forecasts

You can also track any incoming rain on BOM's precipitation radar.

Rain and river levels

Creek and river levels can become dangerously high with alarming rapidity after rain – especially in canyon and gorge environments. BOM provides up-to-date charts on rainfall and river levels: www.bom.gov.au/nsw/flood

The most useful graphs for river levels are:

Wyong, Nepean-Hawkesbury, Georges, Parramatta:

- Grose River at Grose Wold (for Grose River)
- Capertee River at Glen Davis (for Colo River)
- Colo River at Upper Colo (for Colo and Wollangambe Rivers)
- Coxs River at Kelpie Point (for Coxs River + helpful for Kowmung River)

Shoalhaven, Moruya, Clyde, Tuross, Bega, Pambula, Snowy:

- Shoalhaven River at Fossickers Flat (for Shoalhaven River and Bungonia)

Useful hourly and 24-hour rainfall bulletins are also given for locations within the following catchments:

- Coxs River (Cedar Ford for Kowmung River, Kelpie Point for Coxs River)
- Grose River
- Colo River
- Upper Shoalhaven River

Tides

Check tide times if you're planning on swimming somewhere noted as being tide affected: www.bom.gov.au/australia/tides/

Before you Go

What to take wild swimming

Part of the beauty of wild swimming is that you don't need any special equipment – natural water and a willingness to hop in is enough. Still, sometimes a few extra items can make the experience more enjoyable.

1. Swimmers – cossies, budgie-smugglers or togs; whatever you call them. Unless you're swimming in an out-of-the-way place, you're going to need them.

2. Sunscreen, hat, rash-shirt and sunglasses – all help protect against heat stroke and sun damage.

3. A towel – to sit on and dry off with.

4. Plastic bags – for taking home rubbish and wet swimmers.

5. Goggles – to let you see what's going on under the water.

6. A bottle of water – to ensure you stay hydrated.

Almost any time is a good time to go wild swimming. However, there are a few considerations that may improve your experience.

The Greater Sydney area is made up of regions with differing climates, and having some idea of these regional differences can help you plan your next wild swimming adventure.

Climate and water temperature: Sea-surface temperatures fluctuate with the seasons, peaking at around 24°C in February and dropping to 17°C in August. You can swim in the sea comfortably between November and May, though with some acclimatization the season can be extended. The sea-surface temperature tends to be about 1°C warmer in Newcastle than in Jervis Bay.

Freshwater is much more prone to temperature fluctuations due to air temperature and rainfall. A week of hot, dry weather will warm up a river even in early October. By contrast, prolonged, wet, cool weather will result in a drop in water temperature. The water of small creeks and canyons may only reach the mid-teens °C in summer, whereas a wide, shallow, slow-moving river can reach as high as 35°C – much warmer than the sea.

Generally, in low-lying regions you can swim comfortably in freshwater between October and April. For the Upper Blue Mountains and the Southern Highlands, the swimming season is shorter – November to March. Even when the days are hot, be aware when camping that temperatures take a steep dive at night in upland areas.

Busyness: Many locations in this book have been accorded a seclusion rating, to give you some idea of how busy they're likely to be. In all cases, if you're after solitude, your best bet is to swim mid-week, early morning or late afternoon, outside of school and public holidays.

Bush conditions: The National Park & Wildlife Service (NPWS) website provides information on track closures, fire bans and bushfire incidents. If you're heading to the bush, have a look first so you can be informed: www.nationalparks.nsw.gov.au/alerts/Alerts-list.

Camping: To book a campsite in a NPWS-managed campground, call 13000 PARKS (1300072757), or go to: www.nationalparks.nsw.gov.au/Stay

Swims are organised through the book into geographical areas. A detailed description is given for each swim location, with further information provided in the accompanying text box. Some locations don't warrant high recommendation, and are listed with shorter descriptions at the end of each region chapter ('if you have time...').

Facilities

Nearby available facilities are listed, such as toilets, showers, kiosks, playgrounds and campsites. Where camping is available, 'Campsite' refers to walk-in camping with no facilities; 'Campground' to walk-in camping with some facilities such as toilets; and 'Car-based campground' to car-based camping with facilities such as toilets.

Seclusion

Many swim locations are given a rating based on the likelihood of you meeting other people during your visit. Seclusion is rated as either Busy, Average or Secluded, or a combination of these. Urban locations are generally more visited than bush ones, and the seclusion ratings have been adjusted to reflect this – ensuring that ratings are somewhat relative to their type. So, a quiet, urban rock pool may be rated as more secluded than a bush waterhole that gets the same number of visitors.

Navigation

Bush walks are given a navigation grading, from Easy through to Moderate and Hard. It's strongly recommended that you try some easier walks first to familiarise yourself with these gradings. The terrain and nature of the bush around Sydney can be very challenging, and it is not somewhere to end up unprepared.

- **Easy** Well-signposted tracks suitable for beginners.
- **Moderate:** The track may not be signposted, and some navigation skills will be required to choose the correct direction at intersections.
- **Hard:** The track may be hard to find or difficult to follow, and the walk may include off-track sections. Suitable for experienced walkers with navigation skills only.

For walks graded as Moderate-hard and Hard, it's advisable to take a topographic map. The relevant LPI 1:25,000 Topographic Map and grid reference (GR) for the swim location is provided. Maps can be purchased from tourist and national park information centres, or online from: www.shop.lpi.nsw.gov.au

Descent

The total change of altitude in metres is also given. This figure is for one way only.

Walk-in

The time, distance and grade of walks are given. Unless otherwise stated, these are one-way only. So, for instance, for a walk that is 20 minutes, 1km, you should allow at least 40 minutes in total for walking, in addition to the time you'll spend swimming and enjoying the place. The walk-in times stated in this book assume walkers are reasonably experienced and fit, and carrying day packs. Because people walk at different speeds, these times should be treated as a guide only. For the less fit and/or inexperienced walkers, extra time should be allowed. Extra time should also be allowed when carrying overnight packs, or when walking in mixed-ability groups, and especially with children.

All walks have been measured as accurately as possible using a GPS device. However, bear in mind that distances may not always be precise in locations where GPS signals are compromised, such as in steep-sided valleys and canyons. If you are considering visiting a number of bush swim locations, it's recommended that you buy a GPS device to give you a better idea of how far you've walked.

Each walk is graded in terms of its physical difficulty. This grading is based on the change of altitude over the length of the walk – not solely on either. So, a short, steep walk would be graded as Hard, whereas a longer, more gently sloping walk would be graded as Moderate, even if the overall change in altitude was the same. Walk grading takes into account how well the track is made. A relatively flat track that involves rock-hopping, or is unmade and slippery, may be graded as harder than a moderately sloping walk along a well-made fire trail. Walks are graded as follows:

- **Easy:** Generally flat or mildly undulating.
- **Moderate:** Moderately steep or a mixture of both steep and flat.
- **Hard:** Consistently steep descent/ascents, sometimes with sections of rock scrambling/hopping.

Access, Directions and Public Transport

The nearest road-navigable access point is given for each swim location. Under normal circumstances these can all be reached by two-wheel drive vehicles. Note, however, that conditions can change if a road is unsealed, and driver judgement should then be used.

If the swim location is not readily obvious from the point of access, further detailed directions are provided. Abbreviations given relate to points on a compass: N, E, S, W. L (left) and R (right) are also used. With a couple of stated exceptions, all directions return via the same route. Greater Sydney has an extensive network of trains, buses and ferries. The nearest train station or ferry wharf is named, along with the distance to the access point. With bus links, only the distance is given. Note that distances are not to the swim locations themselves – i.e. the length of the walk must also be added. With road congestion and the cost of parking, as well as environmental considerations, it makes sense to use public transport where possible. This information can be used with Transport NSW's online trip planner to get specific directions, travel times and cost of fares: www.transportnsw.info

GPS and symbols

Latitude and longitude in decimal degrees (WGS84 standard) are given. These are universally accepted by all online and mobile mapping services, and will show the precise location of the swim.

Descriptive symbols help you choose your next swim destination at a glance, by providing further information about locations. Symbols include: Long swim possible; Kids and paddling; and Good campsite. The key can be found on the back sleeve of the book.

Wild Swimming with Children

If you're a parent who loves wild swimming you need not be limited by your nippers, because wild swimming isn't just good for adults, but kids too! Together you can share in the fun of exploring new places, get out as a family and enjoy Sydney's beaches, sea baths, rivers and lagoons!

Unstructured outdoor play is an important part of growing up, but with the rush of everyday life, many kids aren't getting enough.

Later in the introduction we list our top locations in and around Sydney for families. Features to look for include:

- Easy entry and exit points
- Gradual rather than sudden drop-off
- Do not involve a difficult or long walk
- Shade available
- Not in proximity to additional dangers – e.g. unfenced waterfall drop-offs, etc
- No currents, rips or swell
- Warm water – babies and toddlers need warmer water

RECRUIT REINFORCEMENTS

Wild swimming with other families offers distinct advantages – you can share child-minding duties, and children love having mates to share in the watery fun!

TEACH YOUR CHILD TO SWIM!

Swimming is a skill that can be enjoyed for life, so why not start your kids early? Informal swimming classes are available for newborns, while most formal lessons are open to children over four. You can also nurture your child's love of water by providing reassurance and respecting their limits. Young children need the extra security of having a parent close by at all times.

GO ON A FAMILY SWIM SAFARI

Camping is a great way for families to spend time together. Living on much closer quarters than we're accustomed, away from the distractions of everyday life, gives us a chance to reconnect. This kind of family time creates lasting memories.

Safety with Children

1. Supervise children around water at all times by actively watching them and keeping them within arm's reach

2. Weak or non-swimmers should wear a floatation device that conforms to Australian Standards

3. Teach your child what to do if they get into trouble

4. Prevent against cold exposure – if your child's teeth start chattering, get them out of the water to warm up

5. Teach your child to keep an eye on their stuff at the beach (towels etc) and remain parallel to it while in the water

Get involved

Giving back makes you feel great, but also results in the improvement of your wider world. There's no need to make a big commitment of time or money – never underestimate the power of small acts to make a difference.

Pick up a bag of litter on your next swim adventure, lend a hand on a conservation project, or donate to a charity.

The incredible places in this book continue to exist because of the foresight and tireless efforts of many individuals and groups. The pressures on our natural places are ever great, but doing your bit will help safeguard your favourite wild swimming spots for years to come.

Here are the details of some Australian groups doing fantastic work:

National Parks and Wildlife Service manage and run the incredible national parks featured in this book. NPWS are helped in their work by over 6,500 volunteers every year.

www.environment.nsw.gov.au/ volunteers/VolunteerNationalPark.htm

Colong Foundation campaigns for the preservation of natural environments, with particular emphasis on wilderness areas.

www.colongwilderness.org.au

National Parks Association of NSW is a non-government conservation group that seeks to protect, connect and restore the integrity and diversity of natural systems.

www.npansw.org.au

The Australian Marine Conservation Society is our only national charity dedicated exclusively to protecting ocean wildlife and their homes.

www.marineconservation.org.au

Clean Up Australia Day is an annual day of action when thousands of tonnes of rubbish are picked up across Australia. Join an existing clean-up site or create your own – particularly if you know of a neglected swim location.

www.cleanup.org.au/au/CleanUpEvents

Two Hands Project's tagline – 30 Minutes and Two Hands to clean up YOUR world anytime, anywhere – makes it easy for anyone to participate.

www.twohandsproject.org

"The world was not made for any one particular generation alone. Whether we like it or not, we hold the land in trust for our successors."

Myles Dunphy

Etiquette

ENVIRONMENTAL ETIQUETTE

When you wild swim you are literally up to your eyeballs in nature. Aborigines, the traditional owners of the land, view their relationship to the natural world as one of connectivity – and for them, all life is inextricably linked. Along with this inseparable bond comes privilege, and also responsibility.

We can all do our bit to preserve Sydney by adopting a similar long-term outlook, guided by the principles of minimal impact and stewardship.

Don't leave anything behind

Take all rubbish, recyclables, food scraps and personal belongings with you when you leave. There's nothing worse than arriving somewhere, keen to jump in and get wet, and finding litter. It detracts from the beauty of a place and can ruin some of the magic. Litter also suggests that the place is uncared for, and research shows that people are more likely to litter if litter is already present. It also poses a serious problem for wildlife – nobody wants to see fairy penguins caught in submerged plastic bags, goannas eating aluminium foil or birds tangled in fishing line.

TIP: Be prepared and bring a plastic bag for your rubbish on wild swim jaunts. Why not bring an extra one to do a quick tidy up of other people's litter too?

Keep your distance from wildlife

Don't try to feed, touch or harass animals. At its core, wild swimming is about getting out into nature; however, it's worth remembering that once there you're on someone else's turf. Wildlife can be sensitive to the presence of humans, so keep your distance and let them get on with their business.

Look after the landscape

To reduce impact on the bush, stick to established tracks and paths and only camp at existing sites. The underwater environment is also sensitive – apply sunscreen (ideally the chemical-free variety) 15–20 minutes before you go swimming. Although it can be tempting to take home a memento of your swim adventure – within national parks it's

an offence to remove anything (i.e. rocks, sticks, seeds etc.). Places of Aboriginal significance such as middens, grinding grooves and rock art are also protected.

Mind your pees and poos

Don't pee in the water, and only poop in a toilet or well-dug hole. Nitrogen in urine is a fertiliser that facilitates algal growth, depleting oxygen levels in the water. Human faeces are loaded with pathogens and can contaminate and pollute water sources. If there are no toilets available, you'll need to dig a 15cm/6″ deep hole at least 100m from any water. Do your stuff then backfill the hole, placing a stone on top if one is available.

SOCIAL ETIQUETTE

Unlike traditional sports, wild swimming doesn't have a fitness or exercise focus; instead what really matters is the experience you have. It's not just the weather that will determine if you have a good time – people can have an impact too, and a few common courtesies go a long way.

Even if you have somewhere all to yourself, you should be prepared to share it with others. Make sure you keep your gear together; nothing says "this place is mine" like stuff strewn everywhere. Similarly, if you arrive and find other people already there, give them some space by setting up 'camp' away from them.

If you're swimming somewhere cosy like a creek or waterhole, stretch out and enjoy yourself – but if others arrive, give them the same opportunity by getting out for a while.

Wild swimming is supposed to be fun, so it needn't be like you're in a library, but try to be mindful of how much noise you make, and keep the splashing and cannon-balling away from other swimmers.

Nudist beach etiquette.

Obviously you need to keep your eyes open, which at a nudist beach means seeing bums, boobs, and… That's all fine – just don't stare. Ogling is rude and unwelcome. It's fine to go to a nudist beach (clothed) and see what it's like, then leave if it's not for you. But if you decide to stay, show some skin! Sexual activity is illegal and also puts the status of Sydney's few clothing-optional beaches at risk.

Best for Explorers

Be a pioneer and discover your own wild swimming gem

Best for Seclusion

To get away from everyone and everything

Best for Picnics

Grassy flats for lazy afternoons

Best for Skinny Dipping

Little visited and perfect for nude or topless swims

Best for the Unusual

Out of the ordinary spots for a dip

Best for Families

Easy to get to places with protected & shallow water

199 Grose River at Waterboard Fire Trail

Best for Camping

Wonderful waterside locations for pitching a tent

Best for Waterfalls

Impressive waterfalls

Best for Style & Luxury

Cultivated natural swimming, often with deluxe facilities

172 Glenbrook Creek Beach

Best for Wild Beaches

Natural beaches, surrounded by bush

Best for Amazing Views

Expansive vistas to knock your socks off

Best for Sheer Beauty

Scenery to make your jaw drop

Wattamolla

Best for Long Swims

Plenty of room to really stretch your arms

Best Easy Bush Experiences

Quick and accessible fixes of nature

205 Dunns Swamp

Best for Jumping

Deep water below cliffs, jetties and rope swings – for the thrill seekers!

Best for Public Transport

Within easy reach of Sydney's bus, ferry and train network

Best for Aquatic Life

Lots to see *under* the water

City &
Harbour

With the sparkling emerald waters of Port Jackson cutting through its centre, Sydney really is The Harbour City!

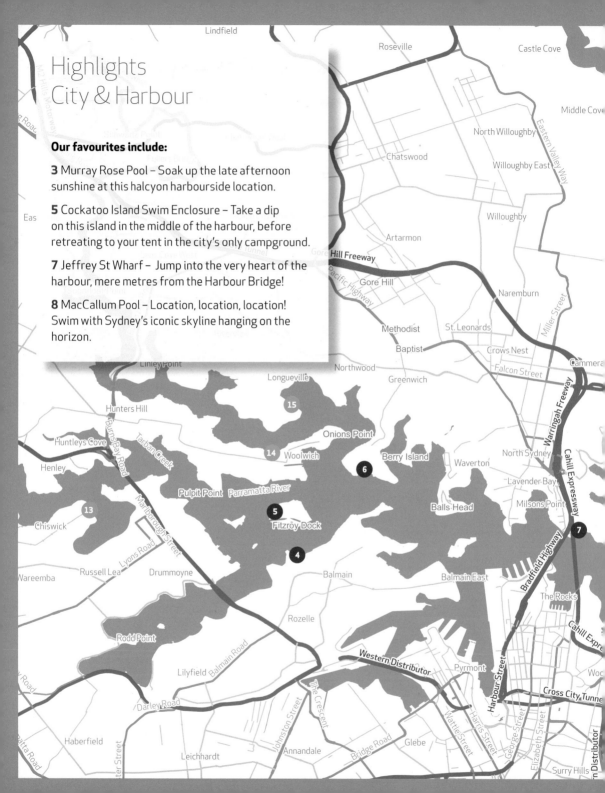

Highlights
City & Harbour

Our favourites include:

3 Murray Rose Pool – Soak up the late afternoon sunshine at this halcyon harbourside location.

5 Cockatoo Island Swim Enclosure – Take a dip on this island in the middle of the harbour, before retreating to your tent in the city's only campground.

7 Jeffrey St Wharf – Jump into the very heart of the harbour, mere metres from the Harbour Bridge!

8 MacCallum Pool – Location, location, location! Swim with Sydney's iconic skyline hanging on the horizon.

Dawn Fraser Baths

2 Shark Beach

Despite an abundance of water, the Harbour may not be an obvious swimming choice – yet it actually has much to offer! With poolside cappuccinos and hot showers, many locations are decidedly civilized; but you'll also find some unexpected, tucked-away swimming gems.

Parsley Bay is a real secret treasure of the Eastern Suburbs. A net encloses much of the bay, and its narrow finger pokes so far into Vaucluse that the water is unfailingly calm and protected. Parsley doesn't have the glamour and social scene that most beaches and pools in this area have – you're OK wearing your nanna swimmers here! The quiet and leafy suburban setting is refreshingly sleepy, and the grassy flat lends itself to whiling away a lazy afternoon.

Shark Beach and Hermitage Foreshore are full of variety, and this walk takes in one of the best beaches in the harbour, a jump rock, and some tiny beaches that feel more tucked away than you'd think was possible in the Eastern Suburbs.

Dubiously named, Shark Beach is actually an extremely popular spot – particularly with the yummy mummies and leathery oldies of Vaucluse. Situated in spacious and shady Nielsen Park, this netted beach is one of the prettiest spots in the harbour, and it marks the start of the walk. Most people, however, venture little farther than its refined environs and even midweek you'll find the northwest-facing beach and its tiered promenade sprinkled with sunbathers.

After Shark Beach, walk around the far headland to probably the best jump rock within the city limits. While a NPWS sign warns of the dangers, unlike at many other sites jumping isn't prohibited – probably because the water below is unusually clear and deep (though it's not recommended at low tide). Exit from the water is via an oyster-covered rock before a steep rock scramble, so footwear is a must. Understandably, it's a popular spot with teenagers, even midweek.

From here, the walk continues through a ribbon of national park, wedged between grand homes and the harbour, taking you past a string of tiny beaches. The water's calm, although sometimes unspectacular – but hey, you really can't have everything!

▶

Parsley Bay

1 PARSLEY BAY

Facilities: Toilets, kiosk at car park
Seclusion: Average
Walk-in: 2 mins, 100m, easy

ⓘ The sandy beach slopes gradually into the 180m enclosure, making it just as good for paddlers as the rest of us. There's also a wharf on the other side of the net that's great for jumping off. Parsley Bay has a lot to offer and it's difficult to understand why it's not more well known.

→ Via car park at end of Horler Ave, Vaucluse. ▣ 200m.

-33.8513, 151.2774 ⛱ ▮ ▸ ▮

2 SHARK BEACH & HERMITAGE FORESHORE

Facilities: Toilets, change-rooms, cafe, playground at Nielsen Park
Seclusion: Busy-average
Walk-in: 2 mins, 120m, easy to Shark Beach, or 45 mins, 1.5km for Hermitage Foreshore Walk.

ⓘ No matter how busy Shark Beach is, its 150m enclosure of alluring cyan never fails to tempt. Of the other beaches, Milk is the most popular, and would be a cracking setting for ringing in the new year. The CBD's skyline appears to rise out of the water, and it's quite an experience to swim here and watch its face change beneath wandering clouds. Farther along is quiet Hermitage Bay, which has a grassy flat scattered with wooden picnic tables and clusters of banana palms. There's a beach, as well as a low, wooden wharf: perfect for jumping in from.

→ From the bottom end of car park on Greycliffe Ave, Vaucluse, walk through gate. For the jump rock and other beaches walk L 300m to the far end of Shark Beach and ascend steps signed Hermitage Foreshore Walking Track. At top, bear R and then shortly turn R down steps. This walk runs S close to the water. After 530m you arrive at the jump rock. Use caution when jumping. After 1km you arrive at Milk Beach. The track then continues through the grounds of state-owned Strickland House. Soon after leaving these gardens, turn R down

to Tingara Beach 1.17km. After 1.37km arrive at the small sandy beach of Hermit Bay. A hundred metres further brings you to the jetty at Hermit Point. The last stop is Queens Beach. ▣ 15m.

-33.8505, 151.2667 ⛱ ▮ ▸ ▮ 🚶 ▮

3 MURRAY ROSE POOL

Facilities: Toilets, change-rooms, kiosk
Seclusion: Busy
Walk-in: 2 mins, 120m, easy

ⓘ A boardwalk runs around the perimeter of the 90m swimming area. There are also two floating pontoons which can be used for jumping – though they're more often sought after as sunning decks from which to see and be seen. It's an oasis of calm in the bustling harbour, and the northwest-facing grassy slopes are the perfect place to soak up the day's sunshine with a good book or friend.

→ Via stairs descending from Woollahra Council offices, off New South Head Rd, Double Bay. Parking is difficult. ▣ 75m.

-33.8716, 151.2471 ▮ ▮

4 Dawn Fraser Baths

Murray Rose Pool. The steps down from the council offices give little suggestion that this netted harbour enclosure and its halcyon-tiered grass suntrap lie beyond. Although far from a secret, the inconspicuous entry means this pool remains a bit of a locals' spot.

Murray Rose Pool was renamed in 2012 to honour the late Olympic swimmer who learned to swim here, although many locals persist in affectionately calling it by its old name – "Red Leaf". The pool takes up part of Seven Shillings Beach, so called because a local Aboriginal man was paid this sum for the fishing rights.

Dawn Fraser Baths. Built in the early 1880s, these baths lay claim to being the oldest tidal baths and swimming club in all of Australia! And they do feel like an old relic – a grand pause in time. The trees in the adjacent park loom above the old pavilion, creating a beautiful backdrop, and it's easy to feel endeared to this slightly shabby but nonetheless charming tidal bath. The wooden walls give it a cosy and secluded feeling and make it a sun-drenched little corner. A boardwalk wraps around it and is perfect for jumping off.

The baths were named after Olympic swimming champion Dawn Fraser, who at 14 was plucked out of the water here by a swim coach who recognised her talent. Dawny still lives locally and we'd like to think she has her own set of keys to allow for a surreptitious moonlight dip!

▶

Murray Rose Pool

6 Greenwich Baths

Cockatoo Island Swim Enclosure

Cockatoo Island Swim Enclosure. Australia celebrates its industrial heritage like no other nation. In no other country would an island of such real estate value be given over to its glory and appreciation – and World Heritage-listed Cockatoo Island is a sprawling 18ha testament to this! More exciting is that a swim enclosure has been made from a disused concrete slipway, where Navy ships were built until the early 1980s.

The swimming isn't fantastic – the water is murky and prone to washed-up litter – but this place is still definitely worth a visit. There really is something compelling about swimming on an island in the middle of Sydney Harbour. Looming above the enclosure and its concrete beach is a crane, and an enormous brick chimney; strange relics from another era. The preservation of the island has ensured it remains an unfussy, tranquil spot amid the hubub of the harbour. Where else in the world can you swim in such a setting?

If you're seeking a getaway from Sydney without actually having to leave it, Cockatoo Island offers the only campground in the city, and there are a host of camping options. One camping area is mere metres from the enclosure – allowing you the opportunity to enjoy it out of hours. If you're really looking to take it easy, you can opt for the glamping package, which includes a pitched tent awaiting your arrival.

Greenwich Baths. These baths offer a very civilized swimming experience, and while this book's focus is on wild swimming, it would be totally understandable if you bought a season ticket! Heliotropic wooden deckchairs and white canvas umbrellas line the water's edge. People quietly read, splayed on flat grassy terraces while kids play on the beach.

The baths are very popular with families and there's even a large selection of toys provided for the kiddos. Greenwich's kiosk, festooned with rows of strung shells, sells gelato, fish and chips, and coffee. If all that's not civilized enough, the baths also hold periodic special events such as open-air movie screenings.

Jeffrey St Wharf. This is the place to *really* fling yourself into the heart of Sydney! There's something about the harbour that mollifies even hardened cynics, such that tourists and locals alike feel cheered by the very sight of it. Here, you're barely a leap away from the fabulous Harbour Bridge. ▶

7 Jeffrey St Wharf

4 DAWN FRASER BATHS

Facilities: Toilets, change-rooms, hot showers, kiosk

Seclusion: Busy

Walk-in: 2 mins, 100m, easy

ⓘ The water is the same heritage green colour as the pavilion, although since it's a few kilometres west of the Harbour Bridge it tends to be somewhat murky, with poor visibility. The water is deep, although at low tide a small beach appears. The pool is roughly divided in half, with a 50m lap area with pontoon starting blocks, and a free swimming area. Entry fees apply. Baths are open October–April.

→ Via Elkington Park off White St, Balmain. 🚌 Balmain West Wharf 450m.

-33.8535, 151.1731 🚌 🍴

5 COCKATOO ISLAND SWIM ENCLOSURE

Facilities: Toilets, picnic tables, BBQs, campground

Seclusion: Average

Walk-in: 5 mins, 350m, easy

ⓘ The netted enclosure is 75m long, and an extensive concrete 'beach' slopes gently into the water, so you can wade a fair distance from shore before the depth drops significantly. Camping fees apply and booking required. See: www.cockatooisland.gov.au

→ From Cockatoo Island ferry wharf, walk through the visitor information centre and bear R. In the distance you see a high chimney stack – the enclosure is located below it. 🚌 Cockatoo Island 0m.

-33.8474, 151.1698 ⛺ 🍴

6 GREENWICH BATHS

Facilities: Toilets, kiosk

Seclusion: Busy

Walk-in: 2 mins, 100m, easy

ⓘ Greenwich is a medium-sized, netted tidal bath with a considerable free swimming area, as well as a roped lane

section with turning boards. The baths have the perpetual ambiance of summer holidays – the kind where sunny days stretch on forever and you only ever leave the water to eat. A wonderful and relaxed place to spend an afternoon. Entry fees apply.

→ Via S end of Albert St, Greenwich. 🚌 Greenwich Point Ferry Wharf 400m.

-33.8414, 151.1828 🚌 🍴

7 JEFFREY ST WHARF

Seclusion: Average

Walk-in: 1 min, 50m, easy

ⓘ There are a range of makeshift jumps from either the wharf or one of the pylons, at heights up to 3–4m depending on the tide, and there's a ladder to help you climb out. Use caution though, as the wharf is occasionally used by tourist ferries. Jeffrey's isn't regarded as a swim spot, so you're likely to only share the wharf with fishermen.

→ Via S end of Broughton St, Kirribilli. 🚌 Milsons Point Wharf 400m.

-33.8499, 151.2139 🍴

9 Clifton Garden Baths

Camp Cove

8 MacCallum Pool

To be clear, nobody has leisurely swims in the deep water of the harbour – it's a little too sharky for that – but here you're at least good for some quick jumps. And anyway, what makes Jeffreys truly awesome is the unrivalled views of the Opera House, CBD and especially the soaring Harbour Bridge – just 100m away!

MacCallum Pool. What an enviable harbourside position: on a Monopoly board MacCallum would be one of the dark blue properties. Tucked as it is below the Morton Bay fig-lined slopes of manicured Cremorne Reserve, it has superb views across the harbour to the Royal Botanical Gardens and Opera House. You may want to mirror the famous arc of the Harbour Bridge with your freestyle arm as it looms in the distance. Alhough penguins aren't allowed into the enclosure, they're apt to do laps in the water just beyond the pool's edge.

Occupying such prime real estate hasn't affected any of the egalitarian ethos that accompanies Australian rock pools – MacCallum really feels like it exists for everyone, and its casual and welcoming atmosphere makes for a laid-back swim. The water is the most enticing shade of luminous green, like lime cordial, especially when the sun catches it (afternoon is best). This is a special place you should swim in at least once!

Clifton Garden Baths. This is a great place for families, with a protected harbour beach and a jetty for jumping off; but what really makes Clifton Gardens is the setting. The large grassy flats are terrific for sprawling out on. Have a picnic, read the paper, or play your favourite game – there's certainly space for it! The bath's net is also home to a colony of seahorses, so if you bring your goggles you might just catch a glimpse of one of these unusual creatures.

10 Camp Cove

8 MACCALLUM POOL

Seclusion: Busy-average
Walk-in: 5 mins, 200m, easy

ⓘ The 30m pool is flanked by a wooden boardwalk, which is raised up from the water, so that as you swim you can spy harbour life unfold before you: ferries zigzag through the water and the white triangles of sailboats glide silently by. Closed one day a week for cleaning. See: www.northsydney.nsw.gov.au

→ Via path off Milson Rd, Cremorne Point, just N of junction with Rialto Ave. 🅿 50m.

-33.8452, 151.2280

9 CLIFTON GARDEN BATHS

Facilities: Toilets, change-rooms, picnic tables, playground
Seclusion: Busy
Walk-in: 2 mins, 80m, easy

ⓘ The jetty divides the wide bay almost in half, and as the sun beams off its surface the water takes on the familiar Sydney Harbour deep turquoise. The beach is ideal for paddlers and children, with languidly sloping sand. Further out the sand is dotted with thick beds of sea grass, whose light undersides become illuminated as they sway in the currents and they look just like a living Gloria Petyarre painting. The water becomes deep (12ft at high tide) near the far end of the jetty, and it's an awesome spot for jumping.

→ Via car park off Morella Rd, Mosman. Open daily 6am–9:30pm. Parking fees apply. 🅿 200m via Sarahs Walk.

-33.8395, 151.2529 🍴 🚌

10 CAMP COVE

Facilities: Showers, kiosk
Walk-in: 1 min, 50m, easy

ⓘ Tucked just inside the harbour entrance, and with views of the city skyline, this is a great location. The turquoise water is calm, and the northwest-facing beach feels like it should be private property, as it backs directly onto the gardens of a handful of posh homes. Popular even midweek, car parks are always in hot demand.

→ From N end of Pacific St, Watson's Bay, take path at 2 o'clock. 🅿 1km.

-33.8397, 151.2788 🍴

Laings Point Rock Pool

Woolwich Baths

And if you have time...

11 LAINGS POINT ROCK POOL

Walk-in: 1 min, 90m, easy

ⓘ **This very little-known rock pool oozes rustic charm. At just 15m long it would feel crowded if shared. The sandy bottom makes for lovely clear water, but it's best around high tide. It's a nice spot to spend an afternoon, with a grassy slope that has good views of the CBD.**

→ From N end of Pacific St, Watsons Bay, descend steps at 10 o'clock and bear R through reserve. The pool is cut into the rock platform. If you reach a tiny brick building you've gone 15m too far. Alternatively, walk around headland from S-end of Camp Cove 180m. Watsons Bay Wharf 800m.

-33.8413, 151.2767

12 WATSONS BAY BATHS

Facilities: Toilets, change-rooms, kiosk, wheelchair access

Walk-in: 1 min, 20m, easy

ⓘ **$2 million was recently spent to renovate these baths, and they're now the fanciest in Sydney. Solidly built with pontoon dive blocks and a pier, the small beach is also popular with families – but it doesn't have enough charm to lure non-locals.**

→ Via Marine Pde, Watsons Bay. Watsons Bay Wharf 200m.

-33.8452, 151.2814

13 CHISWICK BATHS

Facilities: Toilets, picnic tables, BBQs

Walk-in: 1 min, 70m, easy

ⓘ **Small and uninspiring netted enclosure backed by park in a suburban bay setting.**

→ Via Chambers Park off Bortfield Dr, Chiswick. 80m.

-33.8472, 151.1427

14 WOOLWICH BATHS

Facilities: Toilets, change-rooms, picnic table

Walk-in: 1 min, 20m, easy

ⓘ **A 40m enclosure with an old wooden wharf, set in a sundrenched corner amid sandstone cottages with lawns heavy with frangipani trees. As it's so far from the ocean the water can taste a trifle funky.**

→ Via end of Collingwood St, Woolwich. 90m.

-33.8391, 151.1694

15 LUCRETIA BATHS

Walk-in: 1 min, 5m, easy

ⓘ **Despite its fancy address, this is the supermarket home-brand of tidal baths. The 35m enclosure is relatively shallow, but it's a quiet place for a swim.**

→ Via S end of Dunois St, Longueville. 200m

-33.8323, 151.1722

18 Store Beach

Sydney
North

North of Sydney Harbour, you can have the best of both worlds – swim in the serene waters of Middle and North Harbours, Pittwater and Broken Bay, or take a dip in rock pools fronting the unbridled Pacific.

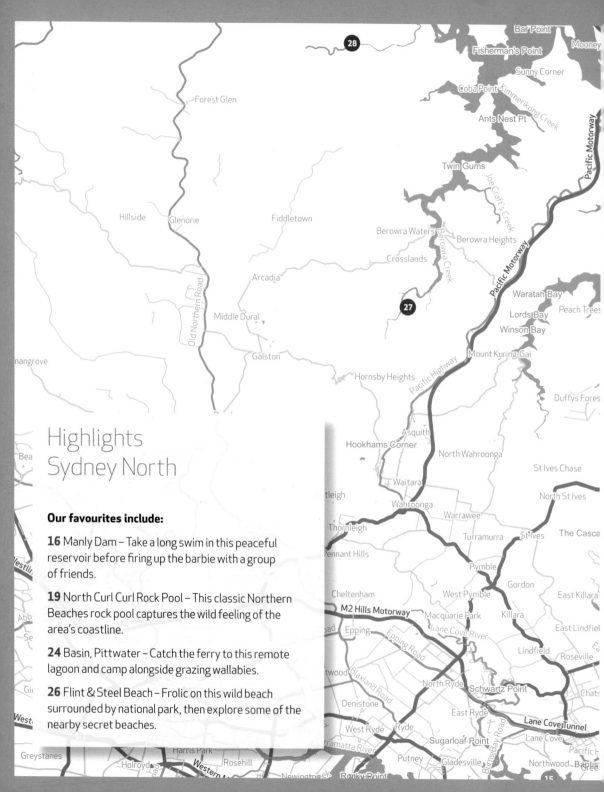

Highlights
Sydney North

Our favourites include:

16 Manly Dam – Take a long swim in this peaceful reservoir before firing up the barbie with a group of friends.

19 North Curl Curl Rock Pool – This classic Northern Beaches rock pool captures the wild feeling of the area's coastline.

24 Basin, Pittwater – Catch the ferry to this remote lagoon and camp alongside grazing wallabies.

26 Flint & Steel Beach – Frolic on this wild beach surrounded by national park, then explore some of the nearby secret beaches.

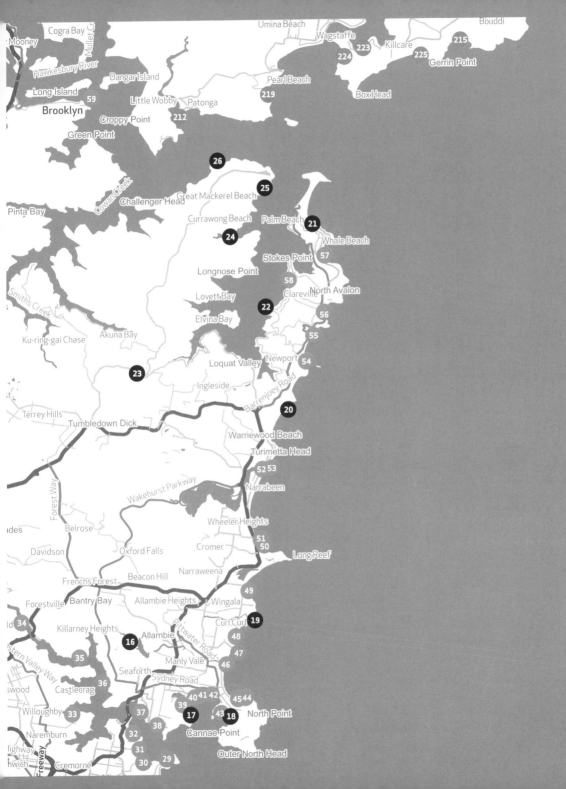

Mooney
Cogra Bay
Hawkesbury River
Long Island   59
Brooklyn
Little Wobby
Dangar Island
Croppy Point
Green Point   212
Pinta Bay
Challenger Head
Great Mackerel Beach
Currawong Beach
Longnose Point
Lovett Bay
Elvina Bay
Akuna Bay
Ku-ring-gai Chase
Smiths Creek
Loquat Valley
Ingleside
Terrey Hills
Tumbledown Dick
Warriewood Beach
Turimetta Head
Narrabeen
Wakehurst Parkway
Wheeler Heights
Belrose
Davidson
Oxford Falls
Cromer
Narraweena
Long Reef
Forest Way
Frenchs Forest
Beacon Hill
Forestville
Bantry Bay
Allambie Heights
Wingala
Killarney Heights
Allambie
Curl Curl
Eastern Valley Way
Seaforth
Manly Vale
Sydney Road
Castlecrag
Willoughby
Naremburn
Cremorne
Cannae Point
Outer North Head
North Point
Umina Beach
Wagstaffe
Bouddi
Killcare
Gerrin Point
Box Head
Pearl Beach
Patonga
Palm Beach
Whale Beach
Stokes Point
North Avalon
Clareville
Newport

223   224   225   215
219
26
25
24   21
57
58
22   56
55
54
23   20
52 53
51
50
49
19
48
47
46
16
34   35   36
37   38   33   32   31   30   29
39   40 41 42   45 44
17   43   18

Collins Beach

Manly Dam

Thick swathes of bush separate this region from the rest of Sydney, and it carries an enticing air of being cut off – although it's actually readily accessible. Best known for its surf breaks and wax head culture, it does have a laid-back, beachy ambience, but it's not just for surfers! Away from the popular surf breaks you'll find wild rock pools, sheltered bayside beaches, and even some cloistered freshwater spots for a swim.

Manly Dam. If you're tired of swimming at the beach and coming home with sand in your budgie smugglers and salt in your eyes, but you don't want to go to a chlorinated pool or drive out of Sydney – this place is for you! Manly Dam is the only remaining large body of freshwater that's clean enough for swimming within the city, and that alone makes it incredibly special.

Originally created by damming Curl Curl Creek, the reservoir provided fresh water to Manly up until the 1930s. Today it's a place of recreation. There are two designated swimming areas: just inside the entrance and then at the far end of the access road, with the section between being reserved for motorboats. The largest and best swimming area is over 700m long!

Reef Beach. It's not flashy, but this former nudist beach has a charm of its own, and rates as one of the most picturesque beaches in the city. Bustling Manly might be just across the harbour, but true to its *au naturel* past, it's a whole other world here and it feels wild and untouched.

The small, northeast-facing beach is swaddled by bush, and cicadas throb with the pulse of summer. Clear water laps the sand, which is dotted with large, dimpled rocks and a few good shady spots – perfect places to sit and watch the ferries go by.

Collins & Store Beaches. These are the kind of beaches that you dream of having to yourself – all that sparkling turquoise water and fine yellow sand. When quiet, they're absolute paradise! So was there ever a better reason for taking the day off work?

Close to Manly, yet surrounded by the dense bush of national park, Collins feels anything but an urban beach. The translucent water is impossible to resist. As clear as glass, you can see right to the bottom where large bunches of golden seaweed sway like the ragged petals of giant yellow dahlias. The area actually has one of the last significant beds of sea grasses remaining in Sydney Harbour. Nearby North Head ▶

Reef Beach

16 MANLY DAM

Facilities: Toilets, picnic tables, BBQs
Seclusion: Average
Walk-in: 2 mins, 70m, easy

ⓘ The dam is the heart of a vast council-managed area of bushland. The bush creates a wonderful feeling of peacefulness, and apart from the distant rumble of traffic, which occasionally rises above the clucks, hoots and quacks of the waterfowl, you could think you're not in the city at all. The large swimming area benefits from a grassy flat with BBQs and picnic tables, making it a great place to spend an afternoon. Water access is easy with gradually tapering sand, so it's just as good for paddlers as it is for distance swimmers.

➜ Via Manly Warringah War Memorial Park, W end of King St, Manly Vale. Open 7am–6:30pm. Main swimming area is accessed from Section 4 car park. 🚗 500m.

-33.7763, 151.2474 🏊 🚣 🚴

17 REEF BEACH

Facilities: Toilets
Seclusion: Average
Navigation: Easy-moderate
Descent: 40m
Walk-in: 10 mins, 410m, easy-moderate

ⓘ Despite passing foot traffic from popular Manly to Spit Bridge Walk, Reef is one of the quietest harbour beaches and makes a great destination in itself.

ⓘ Take track from S end of Beatty St, Balgowlah Heights. After 50m take L at fork, then ignore path on L. After descending steps, turn R at T-junction. Pass toilet block, then shortly afterwards turn L onto beach. 🚗 850m.

-33.8075, 151.2739 🏊

18 COLLINS & STORE BEACHES

Seclusion: Busy-average
Walk-in: 5 mins, 180m, easy

ⓘ While bliss when quiet, both beaches transform during weekends and holidays. They rank as some of Sydney's most popular anchorages and can become bustling floating cities. Unless you have a thing for loud music and swaggering muscles, visit on a mid-week morning!

ⓘ Via car park at end of Collins Beach Rd, Manly. For Store Beach, scramble 400m L around the S rocks. 🚗 800m.

-33.8082, 151.2910

19 NORTH CURL CURL ROCK POOL

Seclusion: Busy-average
Walk-in: 5 mins, 300m, easy-moderate

ⓘ The pool feels very elemental, not only is the unbridled ocean just metres from its edge, but the pool uniquely still contains two monolithic rocks. It's a slightly wonky 32m rectangle, with a rock shelf bottom that changes with the tides. The ocean side is unofficially designated for lap swimmers, who can be found cutting through the water back and forth in stony meditation. Although generally calm inside, the occasional cracking wave crests up and over the surrounding rocks, sending water sheeting down into the pool.

➜ From car park at end of Huston Pde, North Curl Curl. Parking fees apply. Follow "Nature Walk" path starting just to L of SLSC. 🚗 300m.

-33.7676, 151.3018

Mona Vale Rock Pool

is also home to the only Little Penguin colony of mainland NSW, and Collins is reputably a good spot to glimpse them.

Just around the rocky headland is Store Beach. It has the same soft, yellow sand and dazzling water as Collins, but it receives much less foot traffic because it's difficult to access. This makes it feel wilder and more remote, although the distant view across the harbour is crowded with high-rise units.

North Curl Curl Rock Pool. There are so many rock pools in the Northern Beaches, but this one stands out for its isolation and wildness. Stuck out on Dee Why headland, it juts out to be among the vast ocean and sky and quietness of it all. It's the kind of place that you can't get to by accident and its admirers seem to like it that way.

Mona Vale Rock Pool. They say that getting there is half the fun and it's certainly true with this pool! At high tide it's cut off from the beach and transformed into an island. When this happens you must wade knee-deep just to reach its edge!

Swimming in an island of water is a pretty surreal and awesome experience, particularly if you do it at night – and why not? The tall floodlights give the briny air a diffused glow and it's a magical setting for a night swim.

Palm Beach & Palm Beach Rock Pool. "Palmy" to the locals, this is home of the fictitious Summer Bay (from *Home & Away*) and it's easy to see why – it feels like it's on a perpetual summer holiday and you can't imagine winter ever finding its way here.

▶

North Curl Curl Rock Pool

On the surface of it, it's just another beautiful Sydney beach backed by Norfolk Pines and multi-million-dollar homes. Yet Palmy has its own special kind of allure. For one, it's the end of the road and there's definitely something to be said for being the last stop. Although this can mean it becomes clogged with traffic on summer days, it also gives it a laid-back vibe.

On low swell days you can also walk over the rocks beyond the pool to a 2–3m high **jump rock**, which drops into deep, dazzlingly clear water. It's definitely a those-in-the-know kind of place, and consequently doesn't get the crowds of the beach. The water has an abundance of tiny fish that swim between the luscious, waving featherboa like stems of golden seaweed,so bring your goggles!

Taylors Point Baths. It feels as though you've been given the keys to a private pool. A narrow path off a quiet residential street leads to these baths, and backyard gardens almost meet the water. But you don't have to live here to swim in a place that feels your own – so don your swimmers, pack lunch, take a good book and stay a while!

22 Taylors Point Baths

The bath itself is actually nothing flash – just a narrow, 40m, netted swim enclosure with a jetty along one side. However, this tranquil and little-visited spot makes a pleasant change from the wildness of the area's ocean beaches. The far-reaching views over scenic Pittwater to Ku-ring-gai Chase National Park further add to its charm.

Upper Gledhill Falls Pool. In a landscape so dominated by saltwater, you'll be surprised to find such a delightful freshwater pool so close to the North Shore, and you don't need to walk far to reach it. It's only just out of sight below the main road – you'll wonder why you didn't know about it before!

22 Taylors Point Baths

The pool benefits from being enclosed by the beauty of the national park, but is accessed from outside the entry station – so it's free to visit!

The Basin, Pittwater. Despite its relative proximity to Sydney, The Basin carries a wonderful sense of being far removed from it, as the usual way in and out is by ferry. It's an idyllic spot, and the water is as safe as it gets. Come as a day-tripper or stay over as a camper, and loll about on grassy flats alongside the resident wallabies!

A 500m-long saltwater lake cut off from Pittwater, but for a shallow 50m-wide opening – it's not actually a basin, but ▶

Palm Beach

20 MONA VALE ROCK POOL

Facilities: Toilets, change-rooms, showers, picnic tables, BBQs

Seclusion: Busy

Walk-in: 2 mins, 100m, easy

ⓘ Of course, it's not always high tide, and although Mona Vale is at its best then, it's a decent rock pool at any time of day. Even when the ocean around is turbulent, the water inside the 30m pool remains calm. Adjacent Bongin Bongin Beach is generally safe for swimming, usually only receiving low-surging waves.

➔ Via car park at end of Seabeach Ave, Mona Vale. Parking fees apply. 🚗 200m.

-33.6786, 151.3165

21 PALM BEACH & ROCK POOL

Facilities: Toilets, change-rooms, showers

Seclusion: Busy

Walk-in: 2 mins, 70m, easy

ⓘ The beach is a 2km hook of rose-tinted sand. Barrenjoey Headland sits at its northern end – a great leafy dome crowned by the iconic lighthouse. This end is dangerous for swimming – instead, head to the protected southern end, which usually has some of the calmest water in the Northern Beaches. The southern end also has a rock pool. Apart from the water there's nothing natural about the 50m pool, which is concrete, painted and pumped – although its picturesque, north-facing location and far-reaching views make it lovely nonetheless. The pool's concrete beach is a popular and cosy suntrap.

➔ Via S end of Ocean Rd, Palm Beach. Parking fees apply. The jump rock is 120m past the pool on the beach side, near the point, just back from two rock pagodas. 🚗 350m.

-33.6002, 151.3271 🍴🚌🚣

22 TAYLORS POINT BATHS

Seclusion: Average

Walk-in: 2 mins, 100m, easy

ⓘ The enclosure is tidal and best for swimming around high tide, although it's a lovely place regardless. There are shaded benches on its grass bank, which are great for kicking back and relaxing.

➔ From Hudson Pde, Clareville, take path between Royal Australian Navy Establishment and house no. 170. 30m.

-33.6351, 151.3069 🍴🚌

Upper Gledhill Falls Pool

26 White Horse Beach

25 Resolute Beach

24 The Basin, Pittwater

a lagoon. The water is unfailingly calm and there's a shark net to further ensure safe swimming. The sandy floor tapers very gradually, making it a fantastic place for children and paddlers. On the Pittwater side of the campsite there are more opportunities for a dip off a narrow beach, which also offers remarkably placid water.

This is the only place where you are able to camp within Ku-ring-gai Chase National Park. The large, Norfolk Pine-lined, grassy flat is divided roughly in half, with one half for campers and the other for day visitors – during holidays it's a very popular destination for both. It's accessed by the regular 20-minute ferry service from Palm Beach. This is a fantastically scenic journey and travelling this way really makes you feel like you've arrived somewhere when the little, yellow-bowed ferry docks.

Resolute Beach. The water here is so fantastically clear and appealing that you'll want to fling yourself into its green sparkling depths mid-way down the many steps that lead to it!

The low isthmus of Palm Beach extends across the horizon, and offshore boats pace backwards and forwards, with the beach itself being a popular place to drop anchor. This is a little paradise, but arrive early if you want it to yourself!

Flint & Steel Beach. Happiness is different things to different people, but for a swimmer, finding a wild, secluded beach completely to oneself comes pretty close! Such is the magic of this beach that it seems to bring out everyone's inner frolicker. It really is the perfect place to spend a day dashing in and out of the water.

While the beach never gets crowded, it is well known and a Ku-ring-gai favourite for many. So if you find others here and it's solitude you're after, you can always explore the neighbouring hidden beaches.

A track detour will take you to nearby **White Horse Beach** a poetically named and little visited beach. In the 1920s a house stood on the point and the owner used to exercise his horse along the beach below. The northwest-facing beach becomes very thin at high tide and there are a few rocks to navigate when entering the water. It's not as picturesque as Flint and Steel but makes up for it in delightful seclusion. If you really want to be alone, there are a couple of tiny patches of sand nearby which just pass as beaches. These represent your best chances of scoring an entire beach to yourself and swimming sans the restriction of a bathing suit! ▶

The Basin, Pittwater

23 UPPER GLEDHILL FALLS POOL

Seclusion: Average

Walk-in: 5 mins, 80m, moderate (with a low rock-scramble).

ⓘ The 15m pool with dark, green water is fed by a tall waterfall and overlooked by a fern-shrouded cliff. Yes, you can hear the occasional passing motorbike over the noise of the falls, but this is a small price to pay for the location and convenience! There's a tiny sand beach and a few sloping rocks to lounge upon. However, as it's in shade for much of the day and only a short walk, the pool best lends itself to being a stopover to or from Ku-ring-gai, or a short stay on a hot day.

➜ On McCarrs Creek Rd, Ku-ring-gai Chase National Park, 280m W of the West Head Rd junction, park in small lay-by on E side of the signed McCarrs Creek crossing. A path leads down towards creek. Turn R above creek and scramble down a couple of low rock ledges to creek bed before turning L upstream for 25m to pool.

-33.6626, 151.2508 🚗

24 THE BASIN, PITTWATER

Facilities: Toilets, showers, picnic tables, BBQs, campground

Seclusion: Busy-average

Walk-in: 5 mins, 200m, easy

ⓘ Additional fees and booking required for camping – contact NPWS.

➜ From the Palm Beach Ferry Wharf, Barrenjoey Rd, Palm Beach, catch ferry to The Basin, then bear L across the grassy flat to The Basin. 🚢 The Basin 0m.

-33.6053, 151.2915 🚢🛶⛺🍴

25 RESOLUTE BEACH

Seclusion: Average

Navigation: Moderate

Descent: 170m

Walk-in: 45 mins, 2.2km, moderate

ⓘ Stowed away inside the entrance to Pittwater and shut in by steep bush, the west-facing beach is lapped apathetically by calm water – much calmer than Flint & Steel Beach just around the corner.

➜ Follow West Head Rd, Ku-ring-gai Chase National Park (vehicle entry fees apply), for 12.6km, then park in signed car park on R. Take the track signed Resolute Beach. After 400m this passes Aboriginal engravings on the L. After 950m turn L at fork. After 1.95km turn L off fire trail down steps to beach. After 2.1km with the beach in sight, turn L. Alternatively it's a 30-min walk N from ferry at Mackeral Beach. 🚢 Mackeral Beach Terminal 1.2km.

-33.5848, 151.3066 🚢

26 FLINT & STEEL BEACH

Seclusion: Average-secluded

Descent: 150m

Navigation: Easy-moderate

Walk-in: 30 mins, 950m, moderate

ⓘ The 90m, northeast-facing sweep of sand is backed by a low dune and steep bush. Rocky headlands protect it, and although it receives low waves, the water is generally calm and good for swimming. The outlook is green, with national park also visible across the water. Around the far headland is a smaller beach with the same lovely views, and while not as pretty, it's so little visited that the chances are you'll have it to yourself.

27 Crosslands Reserve

Crosslands Reserve. Boasting a jump rock and campground, this pleasant location is an easy bush escape from the North Shore. The sprawling, tree-dotted, grassy flat is perfect for a post-swim picnic or game of frisbee, and makes it an ideal place to come with a group of friends.

Berowra Creek is almost at its tidal limit here and the saltiness is barely perceptible. If you stay overnight, just make sure you're zipped up in your tent by dusk because the mozzies can be ravenous!

Marramarra Creek. This is a terrific place to leave Sydney far behind. The creek and campground on its banks are rarely visited and *that* is certainly the appeal! Despite its relative proximity to the city, Marramarra feels a long way away from everything – particularly the ocean, although amazingly it's still tidal. The campground, while now in national park, was once farmland and if you scout about you can find the old orange groves, established by early European settlers.

28 Marramarra Creek

→ Follow West Head Rd, Ku-ring-gai Chase National Park (vehicle entry fees apply) for 11.5km, then park in signed car park on L. From the car park, the track descends gently before reaching a fork after 270m. Bear R for Flint & Steel Beach (L goes to White Horse Beach). The track descends more steeply before reaching Flint & Steel. To reach the smaller beach, walk 230m around far headland (low tide only). For White Horse Beach, from fork turn L. After 370m ignore R turn (this leads after 150m to a tiny low-tide beach via the ruins of an old house). 30m further on, with the water about 20m ahead of you, look out for an overgrown turning L above a large boulder. From here it's just another 50m to the beach – 770m from car park.

-33.5731, 151.2860 🏖️ ⊛

27 CROSSLANDS RESERVE

Facilities: Toilets, picnic shelters, BBQs, playground, campground
Seclusion: Average
Walk-in: 10 mins, 580m, moderate

ⓘ The dark, estuarine water isn't the most inviting, but it's so still that you can watch the progress of the tide as solitary leaves float up or downstream on the water's surface. The tranquillity is only disturbed when someone makes use of the creek's big attractions – the jump rocks. Located on a bend in the creek where the water's deep, a large flattish rock, partly shaded by trees, provides a great 2m jump. If you prefer a more substantial thrill, there's also a 10m jumping cliff right beside it. Camping fees apply and booking required. See: www.hornsby.nsw.gov.au

→ Upon descending the hill at end of Somerville Rd, Hornsby Heights, enter reserve (gates open 8am–7:30pm), and park on the L next to grassy flat. Walk L upstream through the gate along the path adjacent to creek to far end of flat, past the toilet block, and continue. After 560m you arrive at the jump rock on a sharp bend in the river opposite a sand bank. 10m further on a rough path descends R to a low rock by the water.

-33.6334, 151.1106 🏖️ 🍴 ⛺

28 MARRAMARRA CREEK

Facilities: Toilet, picnic tables, wood BBQs, campground
Seclusion: Average-secluded
Navigation: Moderate
Descent: 200m
Walk-in: 75 mins, 3.8km, moderate

ⓘ Although there's a metre tidal range, even at low tide, when the foamy sand emits a brackish smell, there are deep channels for swimming. The setting is lovely with a sunny, grassy flat, tall gums and a leaf-littered sandy beach.

→ Drive along Bloodwood Rd, Arcadia, from junction with Cobah Rd, for 4.6km. Turn L onto Marramarra Ridge Fire Trail and follow for 4km to car park at gate. On foot, follow undulating fire trail; there is a steep descent to the valley floor where there is a T-junction. Turn L and follow through old meadows, across a ford to the large campground. Access to the creek is at the far end.

-33.5221, 151.0861 ⛺

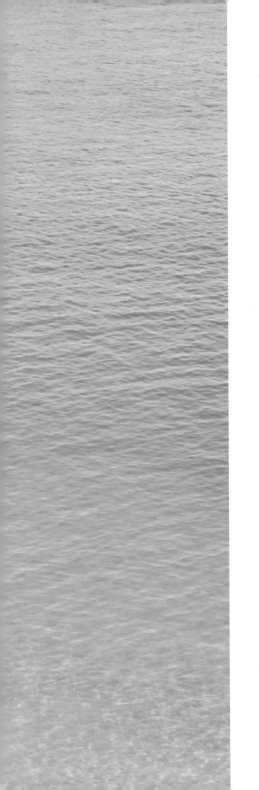

16 Manly Dam

21 Palm Beach

And if you have time...

29 COBBLERS BEACH

Walk-in: 10 min, 450m, easy-moderate

ⓘ Some clothing-optional beaches have an awkward feeling, but Cobbler's isn't like that. The northwest-facing beach is backed by bush, and the harbour water is generally clear and very calm. It's also home to the annual, non-competitive Sydney Skinny Swim – it's super fun, so give it a go! For Sydney Skinny: www.thesydneyskinny.com.au

→ From car park number 6 at the end of Middle Head Rd, Mosman, take gated fire trail on L of road down to beach. Parking fees apply. 📷 300m.

-33.8259, 151.2633 🚫 📷

30 BALMORAL BATHS

Facilities: Toilets, showers, change-rooms, kiosk

Walk-in: 1 min, 25m, easy

ⓘ This grand swim enclosure has a terrific horseshoe boardwalk from which both children and adults drop continuously like lemmings into the water.

→ Via The Esplanade, Mosman, nr junction with Botanic Rd. 📷 180m.

-33.8273, 151.2531 🍽 🚣 🍴

31 EDWARDS BEACH

Facilities: Toilets, showers.

Walk-in: 1 min, 30m, easy

ⓘ This popular, east-facing beach fronts 450m of exceptionally calm water. The sand and adjacent park are always thick with chubby, sand-covered babies and browned oldies licking ice-creams. It's almost overkill, but there's also a shallow rock pool at the northern end.

→ Via N end of The Esplanade, Mosman. 📷 50m.

-33.8217, 151.2515 🏊 🚣

32 CHINAMANS BEACH

Facilities: Toilets, change-rooms, playground

Walk-in: 2 min, 100m, easy

ⓘ It's not flashy, but this northeast-facing beach has a laid-back, Sunday-afternoon charm, which few nearby swim spots do. Tucked inside the entrance of Middle Harbour, and backed by surprisingly natural dunes and a lovely reserve with plenty of shady gums, it's a good place to bring a picnic and troupe of kids.

→ Via Rosherville Reserve, Cyprian St, Mosman. Parking fees apply. 📷 400m.

-33.8150, 151.2487 🚣

33 NORTHBRIDGE POOL

Facilities: Toilets, change-rooms, picnic tables, BBQs

Walk-in: 2 min, 100m, easy-moderate .

ⓘ This respectable but plain pool is set in a bushy corner of Middle Harbour. Enclosed by a wharf, it consists of a 50m lap section and a big, free swimming area. There are large concrete and grassy banks for lounging on, as well as a beach at low tide. Hot showers make it a top place for a winter swim!

→ Via Widgiewa Rd, Northbridge. 📷 700m.

-33.8065, 151.2222

30 Balmoral Baths

35 Flat Rock Beach

34 DAVIDSON PARK SWIM ENCLOSURE

Facilities: Toilets, picnic tables, BBQs
Walk-in: 1 min, 50m, easy

ⓘ Alongside the picnic-perfect grassy flats of Davidson Park is this small, netted swim enclosure. The murky water is often poor quality and it's too shallow for swimming around low tide, but that it's here, 13km from the ocean, is remarkable. The traffic hum from nearby Roseville Bridge is a detraction, but otherwise the bush setting is pretty.

→ Via end of Healey Way, Forestville. Garigal NP vehicle entry fees apply.

-33.7677, 151.2003

35 FLAT ROCK BEACH

Walk-in: 5 mins, 240m, moderate

ⓘ In no time you arrive at one of Sydney's least visited beaches! Surrounded by national park, pink angophoras descend right to the southeast-facing beach and casuarina needles scatter the sand. Apart from the sporadic hum of boats, it's really quiet here. There's only a sliver of beach at high tide, but this provides the best swimming conditions – at low tide the water's too shallow. The beach has a bit of an estuarine look to it and the water visibility is poor, but if you want a quiet wild swim so close to the CBD, these things can be overlooked!

→ Via S end of Killarney Dr, Killarney Heights, take track at end of road. After 40m bear L onto Magazine Track. After 155m bear L again. After 220m ignore ascending steps on L. The beach is just another 20m. 🔲 600m.

-33.7827, 151.2254 ▣

36 GURNEY CRESCENT BATHS

Walk-in: 1 min, 50m, easy

ⓘ An 18m enclosure in a leafy suburban setting, that becomes shallow at low tide.

→ Via path off Gurney Cres, Seaforth, 120m past junction with Bligh Cres. 🔲 300m.

-33.7935, 151.2354 ▣🔲🖼️▣

37 CLONTARF BEACH & SWIM ENCLOSURE

Facilities: Toilets, picnic tables, BBQs, kiosk, playground
Walk-in: 1 min, 60m, easy

ⓘ On weekends the shallow water of this swim enclosure heaves with rambunctious, bucket-and-spade-wielding toddlers. The water at the adjacent, southwest-facing beach is usually very calm, but swimming is best at the quieter southern end.

→ Via car park in Clontarf Reserve off Sandy Bay Rd, Clontarf. Parking fees. 🔲 600m.

-33.8060, 151.2521 ▣🍴

38 CASTLE ROCK BEACH

Walk-in: 1 min, 65m, easy

ⓘ This tucked-away beach is Narnia-esque – so unobtrusively is the path signed, and so unexpectedly do you pop out onto its tiny, golden triangle of sand. However, it's popular with kayakers and walkers, so you'll be lucky to have it to yourself, but it has a real feeling of seclusion that's unusual

48 South Curl Curl Rock Pool

43 Little Manly Baths

so close to the city. A memorably monolithic boulder takes up much of the southwest-facing beach, and unlike many nearby beaches it's awash with late afternoon sunshine.

→ Via end of Ogilvy Rd, Clontarf, take path signed "MSW to the Spit". Cross MSW (Manly Scenic Walkway) and descend steps to beach. 🚍 900m.

-33.8117, 151.2591 🚍

39 FORTY BASKETS POOL

Facilities: Toilets, picnic tables, BBQs
Walk-in: 2 min, 120m, easy

ⓘ In 1885, forty baskets of fish were caught here to feed troops newly returned from Sudan. This 40m tidal bath has a small pier for jumping.

→ Via path off Beatty St, Balgowlah Heights, between houses 28 & 30. 🚍 900m.

-33.8031, 151.2703

40 FAIRLIGHT ROCK POOL

Facilities: Toilets
Walk-in: 5 mins, 200m, easy

ⓘ The water here in this well-maintained pool has that beautiful, green, Manly hue. With a concrete beach, kiddie pool and surrounding childproof fence, it isn't particularly pretty, but it ticks a lot of boxes for many parents, who start arriving early. The small, adjacent, south-facing beach has clear, calm water.

→ Via path off Fairlight Cres, Fairlight, between houses 9 & 11. 🚍 10m.

-33.8001, 151.2756 🏊 🚶

41 DELWOOD BEACH

Walk-in: 2 mins, 200m, easy

ⓘ Surrounded by low cliffs, this tiny, south-facing beach has a relatively secluded feeling, and gets fewer visitors than its neighbours. It's nothing fancy and you have to navigate between rocks to get out into the water, but once in the swimming's good and there's plenty of aquatic life to see.

ⓘ Via S end of Margaret St, Fairlight or along Manly Scenic Walkway, E from ferry wharf. 🚍 Manly Wharf 600m.

-33.7995, 151.2780 🏊 🚶

42 MANLY COVE SWIM ENCLOSURE

Facilities: Toilets, showers
Walk-in: 1 min, 50m, easy

ⓘ This is the first glimpse of Manly that thousands get each day when they arrive at the adjacent ferry terminal. Though not a spectacular spot, the calm water of the 100m-long enclosure is a good place for laps, to cool off or just watch the world go by; and its proximity to the ferry can't be beat!

ⓘ Via West Esplanade, Manly, nr junction with Eustace St. 🚍 Manly Wharf 100m.

-33.7990, 151.2828 🚍 🏊 🚶

43 LITTLE MANLY BATHS

Facilities: Toilets, kiosk, playground
Walk-in: 1 min, 50m, easy

ⓘ A popular locals' swimming spot with a relaxed and unpretentious vibe. The enclosure is 40m long and has a wooden fence from which kids drop like dominos into the deep water below.

→ Via junction of Stuart and Marshall Streets, Manly. 🚶 300m.

-33.8069, 151.2870 🅿️ 🏊 🍴

44 SHELLY BEACH

Facilities: Toilets, showers, change-rooms, kiosk

Walk-in: 1 min, 50m, easy

ⓘ This is one of Sydney's most popular beaches – particularly among ex-pats, and it can get brash and very loud! If that's your thing, the protected water of the deep, west-facing cove is also a great place to swim.

→ Via car park at the end of Bower St, Manly. Parking fees apply. 🚶 950m.

-33.8004, 151.2975 🏊 🍴 ♿

45 FAIRY BOWER BEACH & ROCK POOL

Walk-in: 1 min, 5m, easy

ⓘ This marine reserve, popular with snorkellers, doesn't look like much – just a tiny patch of sand wedged between a small rock pool and the promenade. Still, a myriad of fish take refuge in its calm water among seaweed forests and rock outcrops.

→ Via Marine Parade walkway, off Bower Ln, Manly. 🚶 650m.

-33.8008, 151.2943 🏊 🤿

46 QUEENSCLIFF ROCK POOL

Facilities: Toilets

Walk-in: 2 mins, 125m, easy-moderate

ⓘ An uninspiring 50m concrete rectangle that loses the sun early in the day.

→ Via stairs at the end of Greycliffe St, Queenscliff. 🚶 100m.

-33.7862,151.2894

47 FRESHWATER ROCK POOL

Facilities: Toilets

Walk-in: 2 mins, 100m, moderate

ⓘ This visually uninteresting 50m concrete pool is a hub for lap swimmers.

→ Via car park off Lumsdaine Dr. Parking fees apply. 🚶 250m.

-33.7814, 151.2941 🏊 🐕 🚗

48 SOUTH CURL CURL ROCK POOL

Facilities: Toilets, change-rooms, showers, kiosk

Walk-in: 1 min, 25m, easy

ⓘ Located at the end of one of Sydney's most dangerous beaches is this busy 50m lap pool, which also has a large, shallow free-swimming area.

→ Via car park off Carrington Pde, Curl Curl, nr junction with Beach St. 🚶 0m.

-33.7744, 151.29341 🏊 🍴

49 DEE WHY ROCK POOL

Facilities: Toilets

Walk-in: 1 min, 30m, easy

ⓘ A 50m concrete pool with kiddie pool, fringed by a popular, tiered concrete beach.

→ From E end of Oaks Ave, Dee Why, walk to S-end of beach. Parking fees apply. 🚶 450m.

-33.7551, 151.2990 🏊

44 Shelly Beach

50 Fishermans Beach

52 Narabeen Lagoon

50 FISHERMANS BEACH

Walk-in: 1 min, 20m, easy

ⓘ With the distinct feeling of a local, this east-facing beach is laidback and unassuming – which is exactly why you might like to while away an afternoon here. Swimming is best at the calm, northern end, away from the boat ramp. Visibility isn't great, but the sea grass beds just off the beach are luscious and Fishermans is part of an aquatic reserve.

→ Via car park at end of Florence Ave, Collaroy. ▢ 430m.

-33.7359, 151.3058

51 SOUTH COLLAROY ROCK POOL

Facilities: Wheelchair access

Walk-in: 1 min, 50m, easy

ⓘ This irregular-shaped 50m concrete pool, with kiddie pool, is set below low cliffs.

→ Via N-end of Beach Rd, Collaroy. ▢ 300m.

-33.7335, 151.3044

52 NARRABEEN LAGOON

Walk-in: 1 min, 20m, easy

ⓘ This is the only lagoon in the area still considered clean enough to swim in. Frolicking kids love the shallow water, which covers the expansive sand bars. The water just below the bridge, however, is usually deep enough to jump into (look out for the middle pylon on the lagoon side). And everyone has a go!

→ Via Birdwood Park car park, on S side of bridge, Ocean St, Narrabeen. Parking fees apply. ▢ 140m.

-33.7038, 151.3052

53 NORTH NARRABEEN ROCK POOL

Facilities: Toilets, change-rooms

Walk-in: 5 min, 270m, easy

ⓘ At the northern tip of Narrabeen Beach, a charming, low wooden boardwalk runs around the perimeter of this 50m lap pool. There's also a large free-swimming area.

→ From car park on N side of bridge, Ocean St, Narrabeen, walk through bar gate along pedestrian road to pool. Parking fees apply. ▢ 0m.

-33.7033, 151.3092

54 NEWPORT BEACH ROCK POOL

Facilities: Toilets

Walk-in: 5 mins, 250m, easy

ⓘ A no-frills, 50m lap pool with natural rock shelf bottom at the southern end of the beach.

→ Via path at junction of The Boulevard and Calvert Pde, Newport. ▢ 600m.

-33.6583, 151.3243

55 BILGOLA ROCK POOL

Facilities: Toilets, change-rooms, wheelchair access

Walk-in: 2 mins, 120m, easy

ⓘ This 50m concrete pool, with kiddie pool, is tucked beneath cliffs at the southern end of secluded Bilgola Beach.

→ Via car park adjacent to Bilgola SLSC, off The Serpentine, Bilgola Beach. Parking fees apply. 🚗 600m.

-33.6473, 151.3275 📷

56 AVALON ROCK POOL

Walk-in: 2 mins, 150m, easy

ⓘ Lapping locals make good use of this 25m pool with kiddie pool which, although not particularly attractive, has great ocean views.

→ Via SLSC car park off Barrenjoey Rd, Avalon. 🚗 50m.

-33.6375, 151.3320 📷

57 WHALE BEACH ROCK POOL

Facilities: Toilets, change-rooms, BBQs, playground

Walk-in: 1 min, 100m, easy

ⓘ A shallow pool suitable for children.

→ Via S end of The Strand, Whale Beach. Parking fees apply.

-33.6135, 151.3323 📷

58 PARADISE BEACH SWIM ENCLOSURE

Walk-in: 1 min, 20m, easy

ⓘ 'Paradise' might be a bit of a stretch, but this Pittwater enclosure, popular with families, has a laid-back feeling. At low tide the water is very shallow.

→ Via N end of Paradise Ave, Avalon. 🚗 550m.

-33.6239, 151.3168 📷

59 BROOKLYN BATHS

Facilities: Toilets, picnic tables, BBQs, playground

Walk-in: 5 mins, 200m, easy

ⓘ A 50m enclosure on the banks of the mighty and murky Hawkesbury, with a large wharf good for jumping off – although it's also a top place to chow down on hot chips.

→ Via end of Dangar Rd, Brooklyn.🚉 Hawkesbury River Station 400m.

-33.5463, 151.2313 🍴

50 Fishermans Beach

Little Bay

Sydney East

Right on the doorstep of the city, 30km of coastline with tantalising aqua water and a string of fantastic beaches and rock pools awaits!

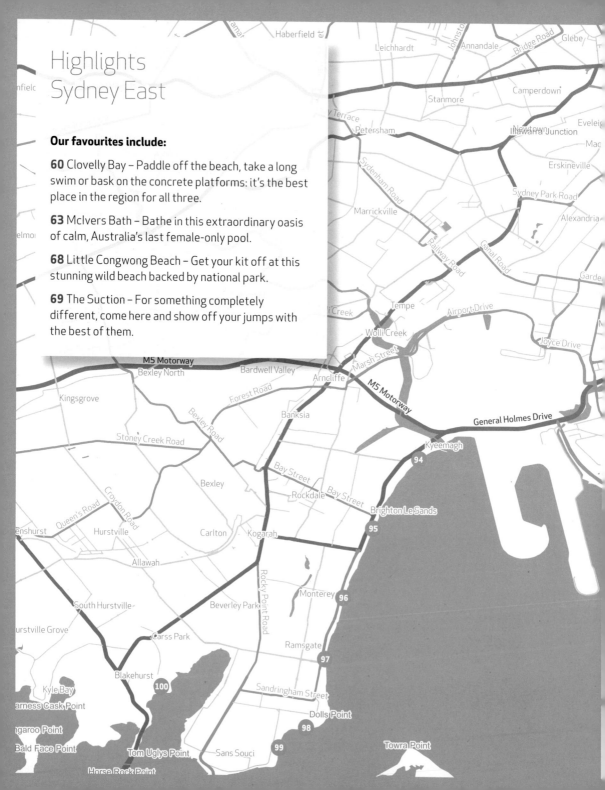

Highlights
Sydney East

Our favourites include:

60 Clovelly Bay – Paddle off the beach, take a long swim or bask on the concrete platforms: it's the best place in the region for all three.

63 McIvers Bath – Bathe in this extraordinary oasis of calm, Australia's last female-only pool.

68 Little Congwong Beach – Get your kit off at this stunning wild beach backed by national park.

69 The Suction – For something completely different, come here and show off your jumps with the best of them.

60 Clovelly Bay

Gordons Bay

The Eastern Suburbs are home to Australia's most famous beach: Bondi. Yet, let's face it – unless you like jumping in the surf, it's no good for swimming. But beyond its waves is a coastline teeming with calm bays and beaches, and overflowing with rock pools.

Clovelly Bay. This is what urban swim dreams are made of – a bay that's 350m long but only 60m across! Such implausibly lanky dimensions make Clovelly the perfect place for swimming. If that's not enough to entice you, there's also its unique sprawling concrete beaches to flop onto post-swim.

A large breakwater beyond the entrance of the bay dulls any incoming waves, ensuring that the water is nearly always calm. The bay also sits in an aquatic reserve, so it's a great place for fish spotting – the most well known of which is the locally famous "Bluey", the blue grouper. There's some disagreement as to whether the convivial fish is actually Bluey or one of his descendents, but Clovelly is definitely blessed with a resident blue grouper so friendly that divers swear he even enjoys a hug once in a while!

If all that's not enough, Clovelly also has a **rock pool** although it seems like a bit of overkill in a place so naturally suited to swimming!

Gordons Bay. With water of such an inviting minty-blue colour, Gordons seems to insist you get your gear off and jump in! The Bondi to Coogee walk skirts around the bay and you can't help but stop to soak in the sight of it. Protected by an offshore reef, the water's calm and excellent for slowly exploring around the rocks or for doing more serious distance swimming.

Giles Baths. Nobody comes here to swim laps; it's all about enjoying the watery wildness! You can rock-hop and search for scuttling crabs, leap from boulders into the turquoise water, spy darting cuttlefish as you swim, or brave the cave as surging waves crash over and into the pool.

Sequestered below the cliffs of Coogee's northern headland, Giles is made up of a rugged breakwater and a hefty, crumbling sandstone wall. Still, it feels like there's not a whole lot separating you from the ocean.

McIvers Baths. This is a little sanctuary. First established in 1886, today McIvers is the last female-only ocean bath in all of Australia. Women don't come here because it's the best place to swim in the area; what draws its patrons into this hidden world is the lovely all-pervading calm that exists behind its walls. ▶

62 Giles Baths

60 CLOVELLY BAY

Facilities: Toilets, change-rooms, showers, picnic tables, BBQs, kiosk
Seclusion: Busy
Walk-in: 2 mins, 50m, easy
ⓘ Clovelly is a terrific place just to spend an afternoon. Its concrete beaches are perfect for those that don't like the feeling of sand between their toes, and it's lovely soaking up the sun here after a swim. For those who do like a bit of sand, there's also a 100m-deep beach, which gently descends into the water – a top choice for paddlers and children. The entire bay is also surrounded by a ribbon of parkland on the well-known Bondi to Coogee walk, and it acts as a buffer from the nearby houses.

➜ From Donellan Circuit, Clovelly, take steps down through park. 🚻 50m.

-33.9138, 151.2667 🏊‍♂️ 🚻 🚲 🍴

61 GORDONS BAY

Seclusion: Busy-average
Walk-in: 5 mins, 200m, easy-moderate
ⓘ What Gordons lacks in amenities and cultivation (compared to nearby Clovelly), it makes up for in charming ruggedness and relative quietness. At 350m long and almost as wide, Gordons is perhaps the best place in the Eastern Suburbs to stretch your swimming arms. Rickety-looking wooden boat ramps and fading dinghies cover the small, southeast-facing beach, so visitors spread out over the jumble of rocks that edge the bay. Council signs declare that dogs are prohibited. However, Gordons remains popular with canines, and dogs lounge waterside, watching the passing swimmers come and go.

➜ Via end of Major St, Coogee. 🚻 350m.

-33.9150, 151.2613 🏊‍♂️ 🚲

62 GILES BATHS

Seclusion: Busy
Walk-in: 5 mins, 200m, easy-moderate
ⓘ The swimming conditions vary a lot depending on tide and swell, but this variety is a big part of Giles' appeal. On calm days the water is sparkling and every crevice on the rock floor is visible. When a swell is pumping, the pool is a mess of white and it takes all your energy just to resist being swept back towards the shore.

➜ From end of Baden St, Coogee, walk 2 o'clock across reserve and descend steps on the beach side of headland. 🚻 200m.

-33.9201, 151.2605 🏊‍♂️

64 Wylies Baths

63 McIvers Baths

You would imagine that the 20c entry fee, which you toss into a bucket, has not changed in decades. While it may seem slightly comical to charge such a miniscule fee, for McIvers it somehow fits. Coogee Ladies Swimming Club run the pool and have managed to keep things unpretentious – even the weekend swimming lessons they offer are free!

There *are* a fair number of bare breasts (of all shapes, sizes and ages), but it's also very popular with young Muslim women. It's an incredible place where women of all kinds feel comfortable.

Wylies Baths. The pool attendant who, with a broad smile, takes your entry fee, greets regulars with a warm,"Hello darling!". On sunny days the concrete platform next to the pool is a mosaic of colourful towels and differing shades of tanned skin. The water sparkles and is dotted with a rainbow of swimming caps, gliding in little neat lines, like abacus beads. Iconic yellow-and-blue change-rooms look down over the pool and provide panoramic views of the ocean. With massages, yoga classes and cappuccinos, wild swimming doesn't get much more civilized than this!

Ivor Rowe Rock Pool. This is by far the smallest rock pool in all of Sydney – a swimmable circle of just 10m across! It counts as one of Sydney's least visited pools, which is a definite plus in the often splitting-at-the-seams Eastern Suburbs ▶

60 Clovelly Bay

64 Wylies Baths

62 McIvers Baths

It's an intimate pool perfect for two, and makes an ideal spot to take in the incredible views of South Coogee, with just ocean as far as the eye can see.

Mahon Rock Pool. Far enough south to avoid the crowds that clog the coast between Bondi and Coogee, this rugged pool has a refreshingly unpretentious vibe. It's famous for being a fantastic, frothy mess when a swell's going, but it also makes a lovely local spot in more sedate weather.

Jutting out on the headland, a thin wall is all that keeps the ocean at bay, so swimming here really is different one day to the next. In calm weather you can swim out to rest on the far wall and take in the super ocean views.

Little Bay. This is one of the least-visited beaches in the Eastern Suburbs, and despite the booming residential development in the area, Little Bay retains a backwater feeling – perfect for that quiet day of sunshine and swimming!

It's the calmest ocean beach in the area, and as waves break long before reaching the shore, it's excellent for swimming. The bay is also consistently ranked as one of Sydney's top snorkelling spots – with numerous varieties of anemones as well as jettisoning cuttlefish. The sandy beach is fairly small, although sandstone outcrops offer secluded little corners.

Congwong & Little Congwong Beaches. These are two of the most natural beaches in the city, and with sparkling aqua water and fine golden sand, they're as close to tropical paradise as Sydney gets!

▶

65 Ivor Rowe Rock Pool

63 MCIVERS BATHS

Facilities: Toilets, change-rooms, showers
Seclusion: Busy
Walk-in: 2 mins, 100m, moderate

ⓘ Steep wooden steps descend to the irregularly-shaped pool, which wraps around the base of the southern Coogee cliffs. Its location means that it misses out on the late afternoon sun – although the grass tiers above are in sunshine most of the day. These tiers are laden with groups of women – most in quiet conversation or reading (though it's not uncommon to see a woman flowing through a session of tai chi). Entry fees apply. Women, and boys under 13 only.

➜ Via steps adjacent to playground in Grant Reserve off Beach St, Coogee. 🚌 280m.

-33.9243, 151.2587

64 WYLIES BATHS

Facilities: Toilets, change-rooms, showers, kiosk
Seclusion: Busy
Walk-in: 1 min, 50m, easy

ⓘ This is a real Coogee institution that's full of nostalgic charm. Its devotees don't simply come here to do some quick laps; instead they spend the day in and out of the pool – swimming, socialising and reading on the large sunning decks. Entry fees apply.

➜ From E end of Neptune St, Coogee, walk N through Grant Reserve. 🚌 300m.

-33.9257, 151.2593 🍴

65 IVOR ROWE ROCK POOL

Seclusion: Average-secluded
Walk-in: 1 min, 50m, easy-moderate

ⓘ For such a small pool there's a real diversity of aquatic life here. Small, shelled creatures bunker down in shallow dips in the rock floor. Black and luscious sea slugs feel their way along, moving by oozing into a tight fat blob of ink, before stretching out and onward. Crabs warily eye you off, posturing with nippers blazing.

➜ Via steps off S end of Bunya Parade, South Coogee. 🚌 450m.

-33.9334, 151.2617

Mahon Rock Pool

The Suction

67 Little Bay Rock Pool

Surrounded by Botany Bay National Park, the southwest-facing beaches carry the remarkable aura of being outside of the city. Around the headland from Congwong is its clothing-optional, smaller neighbour. Little Congwong attracts a diverse mix of browning bodies, and the sound of children laughing floats above the splashing of the waves. Boats moor off-shore here, whether to gain better protection from the nor'easters or to take in the view.

The Suction. If you like industrial landscapes – the beeping of reversing forklifts, the stink of oil refining, the roar of aeroplanes and a touch of graffiti with your swimming – then this is the place to swim. Although nobody comes here to actually swim. This tucked away little corner is where the youths of Mattraville come to posture and perform death-defying jumps off a concrete wall into Yarra Bay. Come join them if that's your thing – there's really nowhere else like it. There can still be kids here mid-week, although as you'd expect it is quieter than on weekends.

Congwong Beach

66 MAHON ROCK POOL

Facilities: Toilets
Seclusion: Busy
Walk-in: 2 mins, 100m, easy

ⓘ Besides the laid-back local atmosphere, the best thing about this pool are the sprawling rock tiers that overlook it. On summer weekends they become tessellated with colourful towels and they're a top spot to catch some sun.

→ Via car park off Marine Pde, Maroubra, nr junction with The Corso. 🅿 100m.

-33.9430, 151.2638

67 LITTLE BAY

Facilities: Toilets, shower
Seclusion: Busy-average
Walk-in: 2 mins, 100m, easy

ⓘ Little Bay was deemed the perfect isolated location for a hospital in the early 1900s following an outbreak of small pox. You can still swim in the tiny bogey hole on its southern rock shelf, which was built to provide shark-free swimming for nurses.

→ Via footpath adjacent to the chapel off Lister Ave, Little Bay. 🅿 550m.

-33.9799, 151.2514 🏖🛶

68 CONGWONG & LITTLE CONGWONG BEACHES

Facilities: Toilets
Seclusion: Busy-average
Walk-in: 1 min, 60m, easy

ⓘ While close to the open ocean, the waves at these beaches barely rise above your ankles, and with water so clear and blue, beneath the surface you could think you're in a vast chlorinated pool! Such beauty hasn't gone unnoticed and they can get busy on weekends.

→ From S end of Anzac Pde, La Perouse, take path before toilet block on L. Little Congwong Beach is a further 300m from the far end of Congwong Beach on a marked track. 🅿 50m.

-33.9891, 151.2348 🏖🚳

69 THE SUCTION

Seclusion: Busy-average
Walk-in: 2 mins, 125m, easy

ⓘ Should you exhaust your jumping repertoire and actually want to swim, the adjacent beach has some of the safest and most inviting aquamarine water in Sydney. It's probably the least-visited beach in the Eastern Suburbs, and sandwiched between dunes and Port Botany, it has its own kind of strange peacefulness.

→ At N end of Prince of Wales Dr, Port Botany, park on L before port gates and take bitumen path on L. After 100m – just before the end – climb over guard rails and descend over the rocks, bearing L to water. 🅿 450m.

-33.9764, 151.2239 🍴

66 Mahon Rock Pool

And if you have time...

70 NORTH BONDI CHILDREN'S POOL & WALLY WEEKES POOL

Walk-in: 1 min, 60m, easy

ⓘ The children's pool is generally ankle-deep and thus only suitable for young children and seagulls. Adjacent is tide-affected Wally Weekes, another shallow pool good for paddlers.

→ Via Ramsgate Ave, North Bondi / N end of Bondi Beach. 🅿 350m.

-33.8915, 151.2823 🏊

71 BONDI ICEBERGS ROCK POOL

Facilities: Toilets, showers, change-rooms, kiddie pool, bistro, sauna.

Walk-in: 20m

ⓘ Probably the most famous rock pool in the world. Home to the body beautiful, its iconic, crisp, whitewashed edges and arctic-blue water are the place to go if you want to see and be seen. The pool and setting are certainly beautiful, but its clique culture feels a bit at odds with the essence of wild swimming. The pool is home to the famed Icebergs Swimming Club, who celebrate the first day of the winter swim season by sharing the pool with enormous blocks of ice. Even in summer, it's all about the laps and you'll find it difficult to have a leisurely swim taking in the fantastic views over Bondi Beach. Entry fees apply. Closed on Thursdays for cleaning. See: www.icebergs.com.au

→ 1 Notts Ave, Bondi. 🅿 180m.

-33.8950, 151.2745 🍴

72 BRONTE BATHS & BOGEY HOLE

Facilities: Toilets, picnic tables, BBQs, kiosk, playground

Walk-in: 2 min, 100m, easy

ⓘ A real favourite among Eastern Suburbs families, Bronte Baths always has a vibrant atmosphere. The 30m pool is divided by a turning board, which separates the splashing kiddies from swimmers. The safest place to swim off Bronte Beach is in the Bogey Hole; the ring of boulders take the full brunt of incoming waves, so that they only ripple over the surface. There's also another lesser-known bogey hole adjacent to the baths.

→ Via Bronte Rd / S end of Bronte Beach. 🅿 50m.

-33.9052, 151.2692 🏊 🍴

73 ROSS JONES MEMORIAL POOL

Walk-in: 1 min, 40m, easy

ⓘ With its iconic turreted wall design that makes it look like a sandcastle, this 18m lap pool, with a kiddie pool, is a busy spot.

→ Via N end of Beach St, adjacent to SLSC at S end of Coogee Beach. 🅿 150m.

-33.9228, 151.2578 🏊

72 Bronte Baths

71 Bondi Icebergs

74 SOUTH MAROUBRA ROCK POOLS

Walk-in: 5 mins, 250m, easy

ⓘ Two decent adjoining bogey holes which are ideal for kiddies.

➜ From far end of Arthur Byrne Reserve car park off Fitzgerald Ave, Maroubra, walk through the dunes to the S end of the beach. Bus to Marine Pde Terminus 650m.

-33.9535, 151.2581

75 LONG BAY

Facilities: Toilets, picnic tables, BBQs, playground

Walk-in: 2 min, 100m, easy

ⓘ This is a seriously massive space for swimming – over 1km long and up to 400m wide! While it does have a nice sleepy feel, and is one of the least visited beaches in the region, the bay's setting is strangely uninspiring. Incredibly, the bay was closed to swimmers for almost 50 years due to pollution, but a lot of money has been spent, resulting in a dramatic improvement in water quality.

➜ Via Fishermans Rd, Malabar. 🅿 200m.

-33.9642, 151.2522

76 MALABAR ROCK POOL

Facilities: Wheelchair access

Walk-in: 1 min, 25m, easy

ⓘ On the southern side of Long Bay is this quiet, unpretentious, no-frills local. Fish swim through the waving sea grasses that line the pool, which reaches depths of 2m.

➜ Via car park at S end of Bay Pde, Malabar. 🅿 100m.

-33.9684, 151.2545

Sydney South

Bay, beach and bush – there's something for everyone, including the most secluded swims within Sydney's city limits!

Highlights
Sydney South

Our favourites include:

79 Gunnamatta Bay Baths – Catch the train with the family in tow for a day of picnicking, paddling and swimming in these baths that manage to keep it real.

81 Lower Kangaroo Creek – Leisurely swim a beautiful 2km stretch of unhurried river.

86 Wattamolla – The place that has something for everyone. Leap from a waterfall, splash in the shallows, or take a long explorative swim in this sandy lagoon and wild beach.

88 Figure Eight Pool – A remarkable natural rock pool that has to be seen to be believed.

91 Lake Eckersley – The tiny campsite beside this sleepy stretch of river is the perfect place to head for a romantic weekend of swimming and camping with your significant other.

The southern suburbs of Sydney nestle between Heathcote National Park in the west and Royal National Park in the east. As well as being laden with fabulous bush swim spots, running the full gamut from coastal lagoons to inland waterholes, it also has some excellent suburban tidal baths. Some of these watery destinations are known Sydney over and attract scores of visitors – yet other special places remain virtually unknown.

Jew Fish Bay Baths. A net stretches right across the bay here, enclosing a whopping 330m of exceedingly calm water. This is by far the largest tidal bath in Sydney – it's so liberating to be able to swim unencumbered in such a huge area without fear of sharks!

Jew Fish has a very different feeling to most other tidal baths: deep in suburbia, although surrounded by the greenery of a massive bush reserve, there's an unusual naturalness here. The complete absence of moored boats also gives it a satisfying quiet.

78 Boat Harbour

Boat Harbour. At the very end of a beach famed for its surf culture is this sheltered little bay. Boat Harbour is an aquatic reserve with unfailingly calm, clear water and it provides refuge for unusual fish from the Great Barrier Reef.

The sandy floor shelves very gently, before suddenly dropping off into a dark-blue haze at the bay's mouth. It's here that you can chance upon some pretty exotic-looking fish, who get a free ride on the East Australian Current.

Gunnamatta Bay Baths. The foaming surf of Cronulla is only a few blocks away from these baths – close enough that sometimes in the early morning the air here is briny. Yet otherwise, things are very different. No swimming between the flags, no smell of surf wax and no gaggles of bikini-clad teenagers. Here it's kids in t-shirts jumping off the wharf, old men in speedos slowly pacing the length of the net, and picnicking families. It's not flashy, but there's an honesty to it that's appealing.

79 Gunnamatta Bay Baths

The other attraction is a massive park which acts as a buffer to suburbia and is a top spot to throw down a picnic rug. The grassy slopes have innumerable large gum trees – home to a community of possums, who you'll no doubt meet if you have a swim around dusk.

▶

78 Boat Harbour

77 JEW FISH BAY BATHS

Facilities: Toilets, picnic tables
Seclusion: Average
Walk-in: 2 mins, 100m, easy-moderate
ⓘ There's a pontoon diving block, and the two small beaches that appear at low tide are excellent for paddlers. The water is relatively shallow, and the sand gives way to delicious, mousse-like mud underfoot, making it best to visit around high tide. Although murky, Jew Fish consistently gets a good water quality rating, so don't be put off!
➔ Turn 2nd L off Christensen Cct, Oatley into car park (gates close 8pm). 1km.
-33.9834, 151.0591

78 BOAT HARBOUR

Seclusion: Busy-average
Walk-in: 5 mins, 350m, easy
ⓘ The southeast-facing beach wraps around the headland to join the sand of Cronulla, and although it can be accessed by walking along the foreshore, most visitors opt to pay an admission charge and drive right onto the sand. The popular Cronulla Beach side often resembles a car park, but within Boat Harbour itself it's quieter and mid-week you could have the water all to yourself. The low dunes behind the bay house a small shanty village. Unlike elsewhere in Sydney, there are even some full-timers and their Australian flags flap in the breeze.
➔ Via Boat Harbour Park off Captain Cook Dr, Kurnell (vehicle entry fees apply (02) 9923 1944, 2WD vehicles must use car park before beach). Alternative free access via 1.2km walk from the end of Sir Joseph Banks Dr, Kurnell – walk through locked gate to the ocean, then follow the rock shelf R / S, until you reach a little shell-covered beach. From here the path runs above along the edge of the dunes to Boat Harbour.
-34.0379, 151.2011

79 GUNNAMATTA BAY BATHS

Facilities: Toilets, picnic tables, BBQs, playground
Seclusion: Busy
Walk-in: 5 mins, 170m, easy
ⓘ The baths hold on to the afternoon sun much longer than the ocean side of Cronulla, so you can really make the most of a beautiful day. At over 180m long they offer a deceptively extensive area for swimming, but the big drawcard for visitors is the wharf, which runs out from the beach to encircle the 50m lap pool in deep water. There are pontoon starting blocks at both ends, although lap swimmers usually chug alongside the far net instead, leaving this area to the jumpers. This is just as well because on weekends it's thick with them! The long beach has very calm, shallow water and is a terrific place for children to wade.
➔ Via Gunnamatta Park off Nicolson Pde, Cronulla. Cronulla Station 350m.
-34.0584, 151.1493

80 GYMEA BAY BATHS

Facilities: Toilets.
Seclusion: Average
Walk-in: 2 mins, 150m, easy
ⓘ With a 50m swimming area and pontoon starting blocks, there's also a

80 Gymea Bay Baths

Gymea Bay Baths. Hidden within leafy suburbia, this large, heritage-listed tidal bath is a real locals' spot, reserved for those-in-the-know! Despite being in a residential area, it's surrounded by a steep-sided bush reserve, which adds to the tranquility of the location.

In its heyday more than 300 visitors swam here every week; yet today it's an unexpected and hidden gem, unknown even to many locals (including, for 20 years, one of the authors!).

Lower Kangaroo Creek. You become part-explorer and part-wild creature as you swim Kangaroo Creek. It feels so good to do a swim journey; to travel through the landscape, totally immersed in it. Travelling in the creek, you gain a whole new perspective!

▶

81 Lower Kangaroo-Creek

The creek wriggles its way through Royal National Park, merging with the Hacking River just upstream from Audley Weir. The weir creates a very rare 2km uninterrupted stretch of swimmable water, and a short bushwalk bypasses some of its bends to reach the start of this memorable swim. Remember whatever you walk in with, you'll have to swim with, so travelling light is key. Take a lightweight backpack, for your shoes, keys and any extras you can't live without. Once committed to the swim, you have to see it through to the end (unless you hitch a ride back to Audley on a passing canoe!).

The occupants of rowboats and canoes dip their shiny yellow paddles in the water, staring silently as they paddle past – as though you are a creature of this creek – with weed dangling from your goggles, and tiny particles of mud clinging to the hairs on your skin. Dragonflies with little, voluptuous red-and-blue bottoms flash in and out of view.

Despite being long, the swim is easy-going, with no perceptible flow and with plenty of opportunities to stand up and have a rest in shallow sections. The water's incredibly clear and shimmers in waves and radiations. Goggles give you the pleasure of seeing clearly underwater, but also allow you to spot any obstacles. In the warmer months the creek really heats up, so you shouldn't have a problem with getting cold mid-way, but a rash vest and hat will protect you from the sun.

South West Arm Pool. There's nowhere like this in all of Sydney: completely cut off at low tide, it's a sort of saltwater waterhole! This remarkable pool is also well enough off the beaten track that as long as you don't mind drying off next to a prehistoric-looking water monitor, you're likely to have it to yourself.

It's a picturesque setting, with thickset, pink angophoras spilling over the surrounding rocks. The last big boulder on the left is good for jumping off (although you need to propel yourself forward to clear a submerged rock underneath).

Crystal Pool. A more magical place to spend a quiet afternoon surely does not exist. This enticing pool certainly lives up to its name: despite a slight blue-green hue, the water really is crystal clear. If swimming in dark, murky water gives you the heebie jeebies, come here and cast off your worries!

The thick scrubby bush suddenly opens up to reveal a wave-like rock-shelter beside the pool. The water glimmers beneath the sun, illuminating the entire sandy bottom and pockets ▶

80 Gymea Bay Baths

81 Lower Kangaroo Creek

South West Arm Pool

sandy beach at low tide which provides safe paddling for youngsters. The wooden boardwalk has been newly refurbished and the deep water is ideal for jumping into. The swimming club uses the baths on Saturday mornings, but otherwise there isn't a strong lap culture, making it a great place to perfect your cannonballs and swandives!

→ From S end of Gymea Bay Rd, Gymea, turn L onto Ellesmere Rd, then immediately R into very steep Gymea Baths Reserve and park at end. 🅿 200m.

-34.0498, 151.0926 💙

81 LOWER KANGAROO CREEK

Facilities: Toilets, picnic tables, BBQs at Audley
Seclusion: Average
Navigation: Easy
Descent: 80m
Walk-in: 30 mins, 1.2km, moderate
→ Via Sir Bertram Stevens Dr, Audley. Turn R immediately after the Royal NP visitors centre, 3.4km from the Pacific

Hwy (vehicle entry fees apply). Turn R again over the large wooden bridge and park on R. Take the track from the end of the car park signed Robertson's Roundabout. This track crosses over a spur around which Kangaroo Creek loops. After 80m fork R signed Engadine. After 375m turn R at T-junction signed Kangaroo Creek. After descending flights of stairs the track arrives at the creek; bear R and walk downstream. After a short distance you arrive at its junction with Engadine Creek. The swim back downstream to Audley starts here. It's easy to get out onto the R-hand bank at the picnic area, just around the corner from the confluence with Hacking River.

-34.0747, 151.0439 🌊 🅻

82 SOUTH WEST ARM POOL

Seclusion: Average-secluded
Navigation: Easy-moderate
Descent: 125m
Walk-in: 40 mins, 1.7km, moderate
ⓘ From the deep water of Port Hacking, a thin finger of shallow water wiggles through the bush of Royal

National Park, and even at hightide only kayakers can charter its upper reaches. Golden freshwater cascades over a pock-marked sandstone bed to mingle with the green saltwater in the very deep, 60m pool.

→ Follow Warumbal Rd, Royal National Park (vehicle entry fees apply) 400m from junction with Sir Bertram Stevens Dr and park on L. Take track 40m back on opposite side of road, signed Winifred Falls Fire Trail. This starts off flat, but then descends steeply. After 1.4km arrive at T-junction. Turn L. After 30m more you arrive beside Winifred Falls. Continue downstream along path adjacent to creek for another 300m to pool.

-34.0893, 151.0785 💙

83 CRYSTAL POOL

Seclusion: Average-secluded
Navigation: Easy-moderate
Descent: 30m
Walk-in: 10 mins, 500m, easy
ⓘ An unofficial one-car code seems to exist among visitors, whereby if you

Karloo Pool

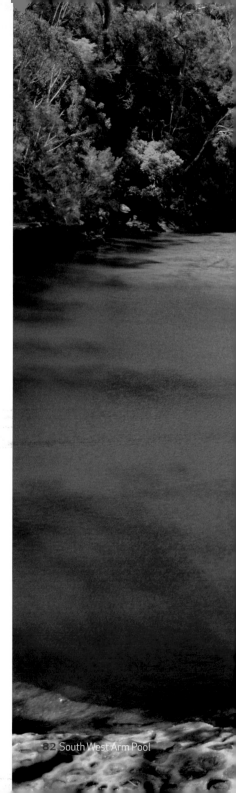

82 South West Arm Pool

82 South West Arm Pool

Crystal Pool

Cabbage Tree Basin

84 Cabbage Tree Basin

of luscious red watergrass. Skaters and water boatmen shine atop the surface like a scattering of diamonds, and are set in perpetual motion by the soft bubbling of a small waterfall.

Cabbage Tree Basin. A saltwater basin of vast lake-like proportions, enclosed by bush and receiving few visitors – Cabbage Tree Basin is a unique place to swim. With all that water and no boats, swell or sharks to share it with, you can really forget about everything and kick for the far shore!

Cabbage Tree is an epically-sized 300m expanse of calm water that reaches depths of up to 7m! This is all the more remarkable considering it's linked to Port Hacking by a shallow, kilometre-long channel.

It also stands out as one of the most serene swim spots close to Sydney, and is frequented by just the occasional fisherman – a midden suggests it's been used in this way for a long time.

Little Marley Beach & Deer Pool. This beach is one of the hidden surprises of Royal National Park. It has a wild and remote feeling, and if you were going to be washed ashore, you could do little better than find yourself here! Only accessible by foot, it's relatively quiet, and also has some of the calmest ocean-facing waters in the park.

From a distance you glimpse Little Marley and it looks impossibly inviting. The distinct colours of the azure water, the grey sandstone, the pale yellow sand, the green heathland and the wide, blue sky are so striking. There are no cars, roads, fences or boats to interrupt the view and that is very rare so close to Sydney. Without all that visual clutter you're almost swallowed up by it all. You probably won't, however, have the beach entirely to yourself, so this isn't the place to frolic naked all day – the popular Coast Track traverses the beach. ▶

Deer Pool

arrive to find a car already in the lay-by you drive on and go elsewhere. This is just as well, as the diminutive pool has a delightfully intimate ambiance and is really only big enough for one group. It's a sensitive place that could easily suffer from misuse, so please treat it with particular care.

→ From Audley, Royal National Park (vehicle entry fees apply), continue S along Sir Bertram Stevens Dr for 7km to South West Arm Creek, drive 400m further and park in lay-by on R next to an unsigned metal gate. Follow the fire trail for a few minutes to its end – ignoring paths to the R. A narrow path continues L / upstream along the creek, through thick scrub for another few minutes to the pool.

-34.1209,151.0707

84 CABBAGE TREE BASIN

Facilities: Toilets, picnic tables, BBQs, hot showers at car-based campground
Seclusion: Average-secluded
Navigation: Hard. Port Hacking GR 274263
Walk-in: 35 mins, 1.4km, easy

ⓘ Camping fees apply and bookings required – contact NPWS.

→ Park at end of Sea Breeze Ln, Bundeena (vehicle entry fees apply), and walk through campground gates. When the road splits, take the L fork and continue to the far L-hand corner of the campground. Locate the footpath to the L of a toilet block signed to Maianbar. After 250m take a path L – if you reach the bridge over the channel you've gone too far, retrace your steps 125m. The walk takes you through an open mangrove floodplain. There are a number of side paths, but keep straight, parallel to the channel of the basin on your R. The path leads you closer to the basin as it opens up skirt around the edge. You'll see your destination ahead – a low rock platform, behind which there's a raised grassy area. 🅿 Bundeena Wharf 1.5km.

-34.0897, 151.1288 🚗 ⛺

85 LITTLE MARLEY BEACH & DEER POOL

Seclusion: Average
Navigation: Easy-moderate

Descent: 180m
Walk-in: 80 mins, 3.8km, easy

ⓘ While not a destination in itself, tiny Deer Pool serves as a perfect and welcome stop-off to and from Little Marley. There's a sandstone platform on which to relax, as well as a small sandy beach. The waterfall can run dry in drought, but the pool remains just deep enough for a cooling dip.

→ From junction with Sir Bertram Stevens Dr, Royal National Park (vehicle entry fees apply), follow Bundeena Rd. for 5.7km to car park on L. Take Marley Track on opposite side of road. Follow until you arrive at Deer Pool (1.85km). Track passes through an old camping area and then turns R. After 2.5km you reach a T-junction with a fire trail. Turn L. Continue to the end of the fire trail and then take path ahead. After 3.6km you reach a T-junction with The Coast Track. Turn R. (L leads to Big Marley Beach, but swimming is dangerous there). After 3.8km, with the beach in sight, bear L down over the rocks.

-34.1206, 151.1358 🏖 🚶

85 Little Marley Beach

Wattamolla always seems to turn it on. Not only is it beautiful, but this wild swimmers' paradise is large and varied enough to satisfy everyone. With so much to offer, it's unsurprisingly the most popular destination in Royal National Park. Unusually, though, even when it's packed it manages to retain much of its charm as you can usually find a quiet pocket. It doesn't get much better than this!

The lagoon is fed by two creeks, one of which tumbles off a cliff providing jumping opportunities for the adventurous. There are a few heights, up to 10m, and while officially prohibited, revelers can always be found hurling themselves off its edge with whoops of delight.

Wattamolla also has a sheltered beach inside the 350m-long cove. The beach tends to get overshadowed by the lagoon; however, it's a lovely swimming spot and is a destination itself. The water is usually very calm, and in 1796 explorers George Bass and Matthew Flinders sought sanctuary here from a savage storm in their tiny boat Tom Thumb.

Curracurrang Pool

If the lagoon and beach fail to satiate your swimming appetite, Wattamolla also has a small old dam. It's a pleasant place to stop while on the coast walk, to get away from the weekend crowds of the lagoon or simply for a fun diversion. Its elevated location means you can enjoy far-reaching views.

Although you'll be spoilt for choice, it doesn't have to be all about the swimming: with grassy flats, a huge sand bank and a shady casuarina grove, Wattamolla is also one of the very best places in Sydney to spend the day.

Curracurrang Pool. This is a special and sensitive place that's been used for corroborees for thousands of years by the local Dharawal people. Today, most visit to escape the crowds elsewhere in Royal National Park, ensuring it has an out-of-the-way tranquility about it.

86 Wattamolla

The small pool is fed by a babbling waterfall, and lush bush descends right to its edges. The water's clear, but levels can be drought-affected. The walk in along the wild coastline is very scenic.

Figure Eight Pool. A photo can't prepare you for the wonder that is Figure Eight – a natural rock pool, perfectly carved into a figure of eight with vertical walls reaching down 2.5m! It's a unique place, made all the more remarkable by the fact that it can only be accessed around low tide.

▶

86 Wattamolla

86 WATTAMOLLA

Facilities: Toilets, picnic tables, BBQs
Seclusion: Busy
Walk-in: 10 mins, 300m, easy
ⓘ Wattamolla is a coastal lagoon nestled in a protected cove and hugged by a wide sand bar. The lagoon stretches for 300m, making longer swims possible, but it rarely gets too deep to stand so is equally suited to youngsters. The eucalypt-green water is usually deliciously warm in summer.

→ From the car park at end of Wattamolla Rd, Royal National Park (vehicle entry fees apply), take the track to the R of the lookout. After 25m turn R. This track leads to the beach and the lagoon entrance. For Wattamolla Dam, follow the Coast Path L from the lookout over the creek, for about 650m. The dam is adjacent to the path on the R.

-34.1372, 151.1161 🏊🍴🛶🚻

87 CURRACURRANG POOL

Seclusion: Average-secluded
Navigation: Moderate
Descent: 40m
Walk-in: 40 mins, 1.6km, easy
→ Via end of Wattamolla Rd, Royal National Park (vehicle entry fees apply). Walk starts from the end of top overflow car park. Take track through locked gate, signed Curracurrang. The walk heads S along the coast towards Curracurrang Cove. After 330m keep R at fork. After 450m the wide track ends. There are a number of false paths here, but turn L towards the ocean and continue S, and you will soon see the cove in the distance. Aim towards this and you will soon pick up the track again if you have lost your way. There are actually two tracks, one that runs along near the cliff top and another that runs more inland, but they meet up later. After 1.4km you reach the cove and Curracurrang Ck, which flows into it. Turn R, upstream, the pool is just 200m further.

-34.1447, 151.1069 🏊🚶

88 FIGURE EIGHT POOL

Seclusion: Busy-average
Navigation: Moderate
Descent: 220m
Walk-in: 75 mins, 3km, moderate
→ From Sir Bertram Stevens Rd, Royal National Park (vehicle entry fees apply), turn onto Garie Rd, then immediately R (unsealed) Garrawarra Farm Rd and park at end. At locked gate to Garrawarra Ridge Management Trail, take path L signed Coast Walk. The path descends through mature bush before opening up to heathland above Burning Palms Beach. After 1km, just after exiting the bush, ignore turning L and continue straight. A little further the path meets the Coast Track. Turn R to Burning Palms; the track descends through the shanty village. Just after crossing a metal footbridge, turn L down steps to beach and continue to S end, then (outside high tide only) over the jumbled rocks, around one headland, and to the point of the next where Figure 8 and a number of other pools are located. It's 950m from the end of the beach to the pool.

-34.1945, 151.0384 🌊🚶

Figure Eight Pool

Figure Eight is just one of a collection of pools located on the coastal shelf just beyond the shantytown of Burning Palms. The shelf juts out into the blue vastness of the ocean, below wrinkled sandstone cliffs, and there are far-reaching views out to sea and down the Illawarra coastline.

The pools are not so much for swimming, but rather for floating and experiencing the delight of the splendid setting. Their walls are lined with all kinds of silky, bobbly and squishy sea life. Some are only big enough for one – not counting the shy crabs you'll share them with – and they make perfect armchairs in which to sit back and take in the view. Larger pools enable short sea-life-watching spurts and some are deep enough to leap into, which is a real novelty. This is a really memorable place, so what are you waiting for?

Bulgo Rock Pool. The story of how this rock pool came to be is as Australian a folk tale as you could hope for. The residents of the coastal shantytown of Bulgo decided they needed a safe place for their kids to swim, and perhaps more importantly, a place to keep their beer cool! A bit of community muscle deepened a natural gash in the rock shelf, and this rock pool was created. The locals would never again drink warm beer, and Sydney became blessed with one of its least-known rock pools!

While cut and carved by the hand of humans, nature seems to have overlooked this and reclaimed it. The pool isn't deep and only about the size of a backyard swimming pool, but its all about the unusual setting. Dramatically situated beneath high, lush, bush-covered slopes, the pool sits at the southernmost point of Royal National Park. The steep walk down makes it the hardest to reach of all the ocean pools, and with the thick, salty air that sometimes blankets it, it feels like you're in another world.

Upper Kangaroo Creek. This walk takes in several bush pools – one of which is famous, the others are little known, but include one of the best in all of Sydney. Don't expect to have beautiful **Karloo Pool** to yourself – it's justifiably popular. The water is deep, but you can still see everything, including the resident eel who quickly shies away the second you dip your toe in. Low rock ledges to dry off on surround the 35m pool, and the bush is flush with banksias and bottlebrushes. It's easily the most visited waterhole in Royal National Park – enthusiastic swimmers rip off their clothes and launch into the water, thrashing out a requisite lap before floating on ▶

89 Bulgo Rock Pool

Lake Eckersley

90 Upper Kangaroo Creek

their backs. Others paddle about with hushed reverence – but if it's quiet you're seeking, best come mid-week or carry on downstream.

Here you pass a couple of smaller pools rimmed by red aquatic grasses. And as you swim, you zoom over twisted tree trunks far below, like the ruins of ancient fallen cities.

The end destination is **Olympic Pool** – the stuff of wild swimming dreams. This 50m pool has deep, clear green water that shimmers kaleidoscopically with the iridescence of an abalone shell. There are plenty of rock ledges for laying out on and a few from which to plunge into the water. Dragonflies pace up and down as if composing love sonnets and the place breathes with a gentle calm. Perhaps most incredible of all is that nobody seems to know about it! Please look after this special place.

Lake Eckersley. Of all the many swimming opportunities in Heathcote National Park, this remote and little-visited place is perhaps the best. A tranquil hideaway, it encourages you to slow down and breathe a little deeper.

▶

90 Olympic Pool

89 BULGO ROCK POOL

Seclusion: Average-secluded
Navigation: Moderate
Descent: 190m
Walk-in: 30 mins, 1.5km, moderate

→ On Lady Wakehurst Dr, Otford, opposite and 10m N of the Apple Pie Shop at junction with Domville Rd, a path starts behind the guard rail beside a short metal post with 1093 on it. After 450m you arrive at a fork in the path where there's a submerged guard rail. Turn L. After a further 50m there's another fork – continue straight "to the beach", rather than R "to the green". When you arrive at the beach, turn R and walk for 250m. The pool is in the rock shelf in front of a few shacks.
🚉 Otford Station 1.6km.

-34.2169, 151.0110

90 UPPER KANGAROO CREEK

Seclusion: Average-secluded
Navigation: Moderate
Descent: 150m
Walk-in: 90 mins, 3.9km, easy-moderate

ⓘ The creek here is characterised by astonishingly clear water, coloured as if it were distilled from leaves of the surrounding trees. It's enough to make your jaw drop – it really is that pretty!

→ From S end of Wilson Pde, Heathcote, take track L, 40m past the Rural Fire Brigade, signed to Karloo. This runs flat behind backyards for 270m before forking off R. Soon after, you start to descend gently, crossing a small creek after 840m. After 1km continue straight over a large, sloping rock. For 1.8km the track is quite level, but thereafter it descends. Arrive at Karloo Pool after 2.4km. To explore downstream, cross over to the rock-shelf on the far side of the pool and follow the path. After 550m you'll arrive at second pool. After 1km you'll arrive at a similiar third pool. After 1.1km the unsigned Bottlebrush Forest exit appears on your L; ignore and after 1.5km you arrive at Olympic Pool.
🚉 Heathcote Station 300m.

-34.0918, 151.0296 📷

91 LAKE ECKERSLEY

Facilities: Campsites
Seclusion: Average-secluded
Navigation: Moderate
Descent: 80m
Walk-in: 75 mins, 3.77km, easy-moderate

ⓘ Eckersley has its own campsite – set on a sandy flat next to the water. It's intimately sized, with room for just a couple tents, and is an amazing place to get away for a restful weekend. Camping fees apply and booking is required – contact NPWS.

→ From end of Oliver St, Heathcote, cross wooden footbridge and take track into bush. After 230m it crosses a water pipeline to reach a fire trail signed Goburra Track. Turn L. After 1.65km steps descend R to Mirang Pool. It's just 50m down to the pool, and another 40m upstream to the sandy campsite. Return to fire trail and continue. After 3km you cross a causeway over Heathcote Creek and ascend a hill. Shortly after, at 3.25km, look out for the Lake Eckersley Track sign R. This arrives at the water's edge after 200m. To reach the campsite,

92. Engadine Lagoon

91. Oak Park Ocean Baths

Lake Eckersley

Lake Eckersley isn't really a lake, but rather two large, meandering bends on the Woronora River. With little perceptible flow, it's ideal for swimming. Voracious, tadpole-sized fish greet your entrance to the water with gentle nibbles. Dragonflies streak up and down the river, and they'll no doubt give you a flyby as you swim through the mirror-like surface that reflects the surrounding gums.

About halfway along the walk to Eckersley is Mirang Pool, on Heathcote Creek. It's a good place to swim in its own right, although its natural beauty is slightly marred by overhead cables. Still, it acts as a great en-route appetiser if the weather's hot, and it also has a campsite.

Engadine Lagoon is one of the best freshwater swimming spots within the city limits. Its mere existence is unusual – a large, clean body of water without a house in sight, *and* only a 15 minute-walk from the 'burbs! Yet that it is so little visited makes it even more extraordinary.

The lagoon is in fact an oval-shaped basin, 150m long, filled with the dark green water of the Woronora River. Set within the confines of a reserve and surrounded by high bush covered slopes, it feels a million kilometres away from Sydney. There are no buzzing lawnmowers or distant murmuring televisions, only the throb of cicadas and the subtle gurgle of water as it winds its way through the valley. Vibrant green reeds edge the pool, replete with water lilies and an abundance of inquisitive dragonflies, which zip in pairs, spiralling in death rolls and pulling up just before they hit the water.

Lake Eckersley

walk R downstream along the edge of the river for 320m. ⬛ Heathcote Station 900m.

-34.0962, 150.9733 🏊 ⛺

92 ENGADINE LAGOON

Seclusion: Average-secluded
Navigation: Moderate
Descent: 100m
Walk-in: 25 mins, 1.1km, moderate
ⓘ If you fancy exploring beyond tranquil Engadine Lagoon, or if you came seeking solitude only to find others already swimming here, you can also visit nearby Little Engadine Lagoon. It's not as large or as spectacular, and there's little space to camp out, but as it gets even fewer visitors it's a top spot for a dip *au naturel*.

➜ From end of Woronora Rd, Engadine, at its junction with Mount Carmel Pl, walk through locked gate and proceed down road. After 175m fork L onto Waterboard Rd. After 500m cross pipeline at crossroad and continue straight downhill, signed Engadine Lagoon Trail. At the turning circle after 1km, take the path straight ahead down to the pool. For Little Engadine Lagoon: 50m after the pipeline crossroad, and just before the power cables, turn L onto overgrown path. This descends to pool after 220m (720m from start of walk). 🅿 600m.

-34.0428, 151.0017 🏊

93 OAK PARK OCEAN BATHS

Facilities: Toilets, BBQs, playground.
Seclusion: Busy-average
Walk-in: 5 mins, 200m, easy
ⓘ Like a cornered-off section of the ocean – half cut from the rock shelf and backed by a small beach – Oak Park feels wilder than nearby baths. It's also a distance from the bustling centre of Cronulla, so this 30m pool is quieter, with a nice locals' vibe.

➜ Through Oak Park off Ewos Pde, Cronulla. 🅿 50m.

-34.0704, 151.1567 🏊

Goburra Pool

And if you have time...

94 KYEEMAGH BATHS

Facilities: Toilets, shower, kiosk, playground

Walk-in: 2 mins, 140m, easy

ⓘ The most northerly of six swim enclosures spaced out along Lady Robinson Beach, on the western shore of Botany Bay. They all have water that is generally calm and gently tapering sand. Kyeemagh is the closest you'll ever swim to the airport runway, and if you (or your kids) like planes, it makes for an interesting backdrop. However, nearby Cooks River affects the water quality.

→ Via path off E end of Bestic St, Kyeemagh. 🅿 180m

-33.9514, 151.1642 🏊 🍴 🚿

95 BRIGHTON-LE-SANDS BATHS

Facilities: Toilets, kiosk

Walk-in: 1 min, 50m, easy

ⓘ The vibrant atmosphere of busy Brighton spills down to the beach and these baths – which are by far the most popular in the bay. The netted enclosure also happens to be the biggest at a whopping 120m x 80m.

→ Off The Grand Pde, Brighton-Le-Sands, nr junction with Duke St. 🅿 10m.

-33.9632, 151.1563 🏊 🍴 🚿

96 MONTEREY BATHS

Facilities: Toilets, picnic tables

Walk-in: 1 min, 30m, easy

ⓘ A large, netted enclosure, separated by a wide slab of fine sand from the popular promenade. There are the usual Botany Bay views, but there's less traffic noise here as the road is set further back.

→ Via car park off The Grand Pde, Monterey, just N of junction with Scarborough St. 🅿 85m.

-33.9749, 151.1512 🚿

97 RAMSGATE BATHS

Facilities: Toilets, picnic tables

Walk-in: 1 min, 30m, easy

ⓘ A 100m enclosure backed by a café and the buzzing promenade.

→ Via car park off The Grand Pde, Ramsgate, at junction with Ramsgate Rd. 🅿 100m.

-33.9853, 151.1481 🚿

98 DOLLS POINT BATHS

Facilities: Toilets

Walk-in: 5 min, 180m, easy

ⓘ Recently renovated enclosure in a quiet spot, away from the main road.

→ From car park off corner of Russell Ave and Malua St, Dolls Point, walk SW through reserve. 🅿 120m.

-33.9969, 151.1448 🚿

99 SANDRINGHAM BATHS

Facilities: Toilets

Walk-in: 1 min, 10m, easy

ⓘ Back in the 1830s, this area was known as Stripper's Point, owing to the local occupation of... bark-stripping! Today, these 40m baths have a quiet residential setting, with bush views across the water; but the beach has eroded away.

96 Monterey Baths

104 Silver Beach Baths

→ Via Vanstone Pde, Sandringham. 🚗 260m.
-34.0003, 151.1401 ♿

100 CARSS BUSH PARK BATHS

Facilities: Picnic tables, BBQs, playground, kiosk

Walk-in: 1 min, 50m, easy

ⓘ This is a large bay enclosure with a sandy beach, backed by reserve. It's always busy with picnicking families, but is a bit flavourless and can suffer from poor water quality.

→ Via S end of Carwar Ave, Carss Park. 🚗 350m.

-33.9902, 151.1194 🛥 🍴 ♿

101 OATLEY BAY BATHS

Facilities: Toilets, playground

Walk-in: 5 min, 200m, easy

ⓘ This enclosure on Georges River has shallow water suitable only for children.

→ Through bar-gate off Annette St, Oatley, nr junction with Russell St. 🚗 180m.

-33.9871, 151.0840 🛥

102 WORONORA RIVER AT PRINCE EDWARD PARK

Facilities: Toilets, picnic tables, BBQs, playground

Walk-in: 2 min, 100m, easy

ⓘ A wide, tidal stretch of river bordered by a flat, grassy, suburban park. It's a popular place with families and picnickers. A footbridge that spans the river also makes a good 3m jump, and recently upgraded facilities have made it a more swimmer-friendly spot.

→ Via car park off Prince Edward Park Rd, Woronora, just before Loftus Creek. 🚗 70m.

-34.0287, 151.0418 🍴 🛥

103 COMO BATHS

Facilities: Toilets, picnic tables, BBQs, playground

Walk-in: 2 min, 100m, easy

ⓘ DH Lawrence noted that Como is: "... a bit like Lake Como, but, oh, so unlike." This 50m enclosure with a wharf is set deep within Georges River, beside a marina and rail bridge. The adjacent chlorinated pool is always busy, but the baths are little used.

→ From end of Cremona Rd, Como, walk through Como Pleasure Grounds. 🚆 Como Station 1km.

-33.9970, 151.0704

104 SILVER BEACH BATHS

Facilities: Café

Walk-in: 1 min, 10m, easy

ⓘ Set between two groynes on Kurnell's Silver Beach, this enclosure is as big as they get. Kurnell, the site of Captain Cook's first landing, is often regarded as the arse-end of Sydney, which is a shame – although on the upside this ensures it remains little visited. So, despite being close to an oil refinery and desalination plant, and opposite Port Botany, the place has a peacefulness and sense of isolation particular to small, end-of-the-road towns, which is rare within Sydney's city limits.

→ Via Prince Charles Pde, Kurnell opposite Village Store. 🚗 50m.

-34.0082, 151.2076 🏊 🛥 🍴

108 Lilli Pilli Baths

112 Goburra Pool

105 SOUTH & NORTH CRONULLA ROCK POOLS

Facilities: Showers

Walk-in: 5 minutes, 300m, easy

ⓘ South Cronulla is a utilitarian, but decent, 50m concrete pool that's very popular with lap swimmers and be-floatied kids. Just 50m away is North Cronulla: despite its central location, it's the least used rock pool in Cronulla. The pool has a rough-around-the-edges charm, with cunjovei-covered walls that become submerged at high tide. Both pools are backed by the pedestrian esplanade and overlooked by tall apartments.

→ From car park off Gerrale St, nr junction with Surf Rd, Cronulla, walk through park to the Esplanade, turn L and continue N. 🚉 Cronulla Station 350m.

-34.0537, 151.1555

106 SHELLY BEACH ROCK POOL

Facilities: Toilets, change-rooms, showers, BBQs, playground, wheelchair access

Walk-in: 2 mins, 150m, easy

ⓘ Loved year-round by local lap swimmers, with a small beach good for paddlers, it sits at the edge of a large park dotted with palm trees.

→ Through Shelly Park off Ewos Pde, Cronulla. 🚉 30m.

-34.0646, 151.1558 🏊

107 DAROOK PARK BEACH

Facilities: Toilets

Walk-in: 5 mins, 170m, easy

ⓘ A leafy, 230m long, bay-side beach that's perennially popular with Cronulla parents. It's a great place for children because the water is always calm, and the beach is so gently sloping that the water is rarely too deep to stand in. In fact, at low tide it vanishes several hundred metres out.

→ Via S end of Darook Park Rd, Cronulla, walk through park. 🚉 350m.

-34.0691, 151.1479 🏊

108 LILLI PILLI BATHS

Facilities: Toilets, change-rooms

Walk-in: 1 min, 50m, easy

ⓘ Quiet, secluded suburban baths, with relatively boat-free views over Port Hacking to Royal National Park. This 38m enclosure has clear, clean water, and thick beds of seagrasses cover the floor.

→ Via end Lilli Pilli Point Rd, Lilli Pilli. 🚉 240m.

-34.0695, 151.1111

109 HACKING RIVER AT SWALLOW ROCK

Facilities: Toilets, picnic tables, BBQs

Walk-in: 1 min, 50m, easy

ⓘ This is a favourite with local families, who come to play in the golden water enclosed by reserve and national park. Although the tranquillity is marred by the adjacent boat ramp, outside high tide a long sandy beach appears, and the setting is quite pretty.

→ Via car park at end of Swallow Rock Dr, Grays Point. 🚉 500m.

-34.061975, 151.078771 q

110 JIBBON BEACH

Walk-in: 1 min, 50m, easy

ⓘ Backed by Royal National Park, Jibbon can have a delightful untouched and wild feeling. On summer weekends though, the water becomes crowded with moored boats. The far end of the 700m-long beach is the most protected and best for swimming.

→ Via path from corner of Neil and Loftus Streets, Bundeena. 🚆 Bundeena Wharf 950m.

-34.0810, 151.1651 🏖

111 KINGFISHER POOL

Navigation: Moderate
Descent: 90m
Walk-in: 40 mins, 1.6km, easy-moderate

ⓘ This is the most visited waterhole in the usually quiet Heathcote National Park. It nestles at the bottom of corrugated banks of sandstone, with a reeds at one end and a waterfall at the other. It has one of only three campsites in the park which, as a rarity, has a toilet. Camping fees apply – contact NPWS.

→ From end of Warabin St, Waterfall, go through locked gate on left and proceed on Bullwarring Track. After 70m turn L down steps. After 350m you rejoin the fire trail. Turn R, and then after a further 15m, turn L back onto the path. After 730m you cross a fire trail again – turn L over the creek bed and then immediately R. After 1.6km you pass the campsite on R, and then shortly afterward you arrive above the pool. 🚆 Waterfall Station 750m.

-34.1263, 150.9774 ⛺

112 GOBURRA POOL

Navigation: Easy-moderate
Descent: 110m
Walk-in: 20 mins, 545m, moderate

ⓘ In a little over 500m, you're transported from the suburbs of Sydney to this idyllic pool, enveloped by the mature bush of Heathcote National Park. With both shady and sun-drenched ledges to camp out on, it's a lovely place to spend the day.

→ From western end of Oliver St, Heathcote, cross over wooden footbridge and follow path downhill. After 230m cross over the water pipeline to reach the Goburra Track junction. Turn R. After another 250m turn sharp L down steps. The pool is just another 65m. 🚆 Heathcote Station 900m.

-34.0795, 150.9978

111 Kingfisher Pool

Illawarra

This area has a magic of its own – locked between sea and escarpment, its scenery is striking and unforgettable.

Highlights
Illawarra

Our favourites include:

114 Jump Rock – Test your daring by leaping into this bottomless waterhole.

116 Gerringong Falls – Nothing speaks of the region's beauty like its magnificent waterfalls – here you can swim in a waterhole just metres from the top of these little-visited, yet gasp-worthy falls.

115 Stone Bridge Pool – Swim among twittering birds and fragrant flowers in this pretty little pool.

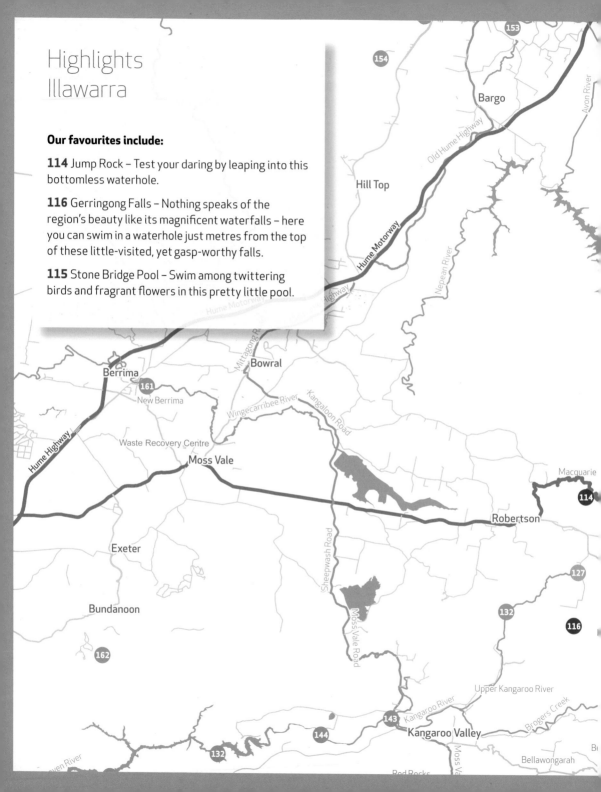

Nuns Pool

Bass Point Reserve, Maloneys Beach

The Illawarra is the coastal region beginning at Sydney's southern edge. Although the region's industrial roots are sometimes evident in the landscape, there's plenty of natural beauty too, with wonderfully sheltered coves nestling in its rocky coastline, and thrilling waterfalls and sculptured canyons hidden in its hinterland.

Nuns Pool. Forgotten and hidden in the shadow of Wollongong Head Lighthouse, you actually have to jump the fence to get down to this pool. The local council have abandoned it and would probably rather you didn't swim here; but what a shame because it's fantastic!

Nuns feels remote considering it's in the middle of a city! The unmanicured nature of it – all pebbles and craggy rock walls, make it feel about as wild as a ocean pool can!

Jump Rock. Fittingly named, people come here to catapult themselves into an impossibly deep pool. It's a popular place, although its location remains a bit of a coveted secret. And if testing your daring isn't your thing, it also happens to be a gorgeous setting for a swim!

A knotted rope enables would-be jumpers to get from the pool to the launching points. From here it's just a matter of psyching yourself up before stepping out and off the edge. Whoosh! It's exhilarating, and the rumbling cascades are so loud that any girly screams that might slip out mid-jump, should be obscured.

Stone Bridge Pool. A natural bridge spans the creek above this lovely pool in Barren Grounds Nature Reserve, creating a charming sun-drenched spot to spend a lazy day. Far from being barren, the surrounds are a rich mix of heathland and open forest, with a reported 180 species of birds and a profusion of wildflowers in spring.

Gerringong Falls. Hyperbole is wholly justified with this pool – it truly is a spectacular place to swim. A lovely pool, unbelievably just metres from where the falls plummet 180m, down, down, down into Kangaroo Valley below. Perching on the edge, the view is awe-inspiring. And there's no safety barriers, warning signs or even other photo-snapping visitors to spoil the moment!

Surrounded by the low heathland of Budderoo National Park, flush with black cockatoos, echidnas and wallabies, the pool is hemmed by partially submerged rock ledges. Just 20m before the epic drop-off, it suddenly loses depth and tadpoles ▶

115 Stone Bridge Pool

113 NUNS POOL

Seclusion: Average-secluded
Walk-in: 5 mins, 120m, moderate

ⓘ Two small walls connect a large rock that guards the entrance to a natural channel, less than 10m wide. The pool is one of the oldest in NSW, built in the 1830s for the wives of officers responsible for marshalling convicts. These days, very few venture down to the pool, and while the water is only just deep enough to swim, you should have this unique and special place to yourself.

→ From car park adjacent to the headland lighthouse (not the harbour one), on Endeavour Dr, Wollongong, walk over to the railings beside the lighthouse to look down into the tiny cove that the pool is in. Walk R to the point lookout, climb over the railings and follow path down L to the beach. 🚶 500m.

-34.4221, 150.9101

114 JUMP ROCK

Seclusion: Busy-average
Navigation: Moderate
Ascent: 90m
Walk-in: 45 mins, 1.77km, moderate

ⓘ Among dominating walls that curve down to meet the water in a lush, narrow valley of Macquarie Pass National Park is a cliff offering jumps between 3–10m. Beneath is this deep pool, hollowed out by the tumbling rivulet.

→ Drive E 9.4km from Albion Park on Illawarra Hwy, then turn L into car park at the entrance to Macquarie Pass National Park, which lies at the very bottom of the pass. Walk through the locked gate and proceed along the trail. Use caution as the track is often wet and slippery. After 430m turn R over an old fallen trunk before a causeway. This path runs upstream parallel to Macquarie Rivulet. After 1.7km cross a small creek that comes in from the R. The pool and jump rock are just another 75m.

-34.5705, 150.6616 🍽

115 STONE BRIDGE POOL

Seclusion: Average
Navigation: Easy
Descent: 50m
Walk-in: 35 mins, 2.1km, easy

ⓘ Lamonds Creek flows cool and slow under the old creek bed before cascading into the pool. Pretty slopes, thick with bracken and ferns, fringe its earthy-tasting, dark orange water. There's also a remarkable 2m-deep pothole in the old creek bed, which makes a perfect pool for one… or two.

→ From Jamberoo travel W for 9.2km on Jamberoo Mountain Rd, then turn sharp L into Barren Grounds Nature Reserve. Park in the picnic area and take locked Griffiths Trail gate ahead – rather than to the L. Continue along fire trail, following signs to Stone Bridge. After 1km turn L at signpost marked Stone Bridge 1km. After 2.1km you arrive at a turning circle. Take path L, it's just another 30m.

-34.6863, 150.7190

118 Blowhole Point Rock Pool

Jump Rock

bunker down in wet grooves in the rock. It's a stunning place to spend the day, drinking in the view and tranquility as you watch butterflies drift up from below the falls and hover over you as you swim.

Bass Point Reserve. This rugged knob of volcanic rock pokes 1.5km into the ocean. Three of its coves are excellent for swimming and a diverse array of marine life can be found sheltering in their protected waters. It also has cultural significance as one of the oldest Aboriginal occupation sites on the East Coast.

A tiny patch of white sand meets the most alluring shade of translucent water – it's not surprising that **Red Sands Beach** is the most popular beach in the reserve. Waves are completely barred from reaching the sand by a collection of rocks and the shallow water is great for pottering swims. The north-facing beach is backed by a luscious band of grass – an ideal place to throw down a picnic rug and spend the day with the family. There's also a small, **natural tidal pool** 150m past the beach.

Nearby, east-facing **Maloney's Beach** doesn't have a wild or secluded feeling, but it makes a strangely beautiful setting for a swim. The shimmering water is rimmed by rocks, and tall, waving pampas stems separate the beach from low grass-hills and the dramatic peaks of Bass Point Quarry.

▶

117 Bass Point Reserve, Red Sands Beach

116 Gerringong Falls

Bass Point Reserve, Bushrangers Bay

At the end of the road is the evocatively named **Bushrangers Bay** – this 400m-long gash in the headland is at times only 40m across, making it very protected. Walking barefoot across the east-facing, small pebble beach will make you wince, but the pain is worth it once you make it in. The brilliant jade-coloured water is deep, with remarkable visibility, and you should keep your eyes open because it's both an aquatic reserve and grey nurse shark habitat. You don't have to worry about being too alert though, because despite appearances, the massive, jagged-toothed creatures aren't the bitey kind!

Blowhole Point Rock Pool. This is by far the best pool in the area. Constructed in 1888, with walls only built where necessary, its natural appearance and feeling make it special. There's not a strong lap culture here.

While not a destination in itself, if you can't quite yet face the bustle of the city, it's *the* place to stop off for an ice-cream and a quick cool down on that long road back from Jervis Bay.

116 Gerringong Falls

116 GERRINGONG FALLS

Seclusion: Secluded
Navigation: Moderate
Descent: 110m
Walk-in: 135 mins, 8.6km, easy

ⓘ The journey here is both blessing and beast. At over 8km one way, it's a long slog – although easy work for those with mountain bikes. However, the remoteness increases your chances of having this amazing spot to yourself, and Gerringong counts as one of the least visited of all the waterfalls of this region. Caution must be taken near the head of the falls. The dangerous location makes it unsuitable for children.

➔ From Jamberoo Mountain Rd, 11km S of Robertson / 12km W of Jamberoo, turn onto Budderoo Plateau Fire Trail and drive for 400m to car park. Proceed on foot through the locked gate. The trail winds its way gently through a mosaic of heathland and mature bush. After 5.8km turn R through another locked gate onto Hersey Fire Trail. After 8.2km the trail ends at a turning circle; continue straight on the narrower track. This brings you, after a few hundred metres, to a creek. Turn L, downstream, initially on the creek bed, before picking up a faint path on the bank. There is a decent, long, narrow pool that cuts across the creek. Soon after, you arrive at the main pool with the falls on your L. Cross over the creek to reach an exposed area of rock near the cliff top.

-34.6612, 150.6530 👣🅿️🚻

117 BASS POINT RESERVE

Seclusion: Busy-average
Walk-in: Easy

➔ Via end of Bass Point Tourist Rd, Shell Cove. Gates open 6.30am–8pm.

➔ For **Red Sands Beach**, turn L 220m after entry gates and take path in far R corner of car park. Follow 150m to beach.

-34.5936, 150.8883 🏖️

➔ For **Maloneys Beach**, turn R 350m after entry gates and take path from far R corner of car park. Follow 150m to beach.

-34.5984, 150.8872

➔ For **Bushrangers Bay**, turn R 1.5km from entry gates and park at end. Take path that leads L, 100m to beach.

-34.5973, 150.8995 🏊🤿🚣

118 BLOWHOLE POINT ROCK POOL

Facilities: Toilets, change-rooms, shower
Seclusion: Busy
Walk-in: 1 min, 50m, easy

➔ From Blowhole Point Rd, Kiama, take first L and park at top of the hill near Norfolk Pines. 🚉 Kiama Station 900m.

-34.6699, 150.8622

Bass Point Reserve, Bushrangers Bay.

And if you have time...

119 WOMBARRA ROCK POOL
Facilities: Toilets, playground
Walk-in: 1 min, 20m, easy
ⓘ An irregular-shaped, 40m concrete pool, with adjoining kiddie pool. A quiet setting backed by a large grassy park.
→ Via end of Reef Ave, Wombarra. 🚉 Wombarra Station 900m.
-34.2801, 150.9560 🐾

120 COLEDALE ROCK POOL
Facilities: Toilets, kiddie pool
Walk-in: 2 min, 100m, easy
ⓘ A 'wilder' feeling 50m concrete pool that's cut out of the rock shelf, which at high tide is covered in ankle-deep water.
→ Via path at end of Northcote St, Coledale. 🚉 Coledale Station 400m.
-34.2918, 150.9466

121 AUSTINMER ROCK POOLS
Facilities: Toilets, change-rooms, showers
Walk-in: 2 mins, 150m, easy

ⓘ A 50m lap pool and 25m free-swimming area. Parking can be difficult.
→ Via car park off Lawrence Hargreave Dr, Austinmer. Pools at S end of beach. 🚉 Austinmer Station 500m.
-34.3079, 150.9350

122 BULLI ROCK POOL
Facilities: Toilets, picnic tables, café
Walk-in: 2 mins, 100m, easy
ⓘ A 50m concrete pool with kiddie pool, set into the rocky headland and backed by a grassy reserve.
→ Via SLSC car park off Trinity Row, Bulli. 🚉 Bulli Station 1.4km.
-34.3395, 150.9264 🐾 🍴 🐾

123 WOONONA ROCK POOL
Facilities: Toilets.
Walk-in: 1 min, 40m, easy
ⓘ A 50m, painted concrete pool, bordered by a wide concrete beach.
→ Via car park at end of Kurraba Rd, Wonoona. 🚉 Wonoona Station 850m.
-34.3474, 150.9232

124 BELLAMBI ROCK POOL
Facilities: Toilets, showers, picnic tables, BBQs, playground, wheelchair access
Walk-in: 1 min, 25m, easy
ⓘ A 50m, concrete pool and kiddie pool, with a concrete beach and grassy flat.
→ Via car park at end of second left off Robert Cram Dr, Bellambi. 🚉 350m.
-34.3656, 150.9241 🐾 🏃

125 TOWRADGI ROCK POOL
Facilities: Toilets, picnic tables, playground, wheelchair access
Walk-in: 1 min, 50m, easy
ⓘ A 50m, painted concrete pool and kiddie pool on a rocky headland. A deep concrete beach with descending tiers.
→ Via E end Towradgi Rd, Towradgi. 🚉 150m
-34.3859, 150.9153 🐾 🏃

126 NORTH WOLLONGONG ROCK POOL
Walk-in: 2 mins, 150m, easy
ⓘ 30m rock pool first constructed in 1890. The surrounding rock shelf is covered at high tide. Adjacent Continental

131 Coalcliff Rock Pool

127 Carrington Falls

Pool is indistinguishable from a municipal chlorinated pool, except that it's salt-water.

→ From Cliff Rd nr. Georges Pl junction, Wollongong, descend steps to Continental Pool. Turn L and walk 100m. 100m.

-34.4178, 150.9027

127 CARRINGTON FALLS & NELLIES GLEN

Facilities: Toilets, picnic tables
Walk-in: 1 min, 40m, easy

ⓘ Spectacular popular falls where, on sunny days, people spread out over rock ledges. There's a languid pool for swimming, shallows for paddling and pot holes for jacuzzis. A pretty, waterfall flows into nearby Nellies Glen – a good-sized pool that sits in a shadowy, fern-covered bowl. Even in summer, the water's chilly. Take care, especially with children, near falls.

→ Turn off Jamberoo Mountain Rd (5km E of Robertson or 21km W of Albion Pk) onto Carrington Falls Rd. After 1.5km R onto unsealed road signed Nellies Glen Picnic Area. After 1.8km park on L, just after causeway. For Nellies Glen (-34.6214,

150.6547), continue 100m further to car park. Through locked gate and follow path to pool, 100m.

-34.6237, 150.6561

128 SHELLHARBOUR ROCK POOL

Facilities: Toilets, picnic tables
Walk-in: 1 min, 15m, easy

ⓘ A sea water Olympic pool – a concrete rectangle and adjoining kiddie pool, with icy-blue water and lane lines.

→ Via car park at junction of Darley St and John St, Shellharbour. 240m.

-34.5794, 150.8723

129 THE BONEYARD

Walk-in: 5 mins, 200m, easy-moderate

ⓘ Don't let the name put you off – this pebble beach is beautiful in a rough-around-the-edges kind of way. The calm bay was a loading dock for nearby Bombo quarry – and there are still unusual geological remnants. The beach is tucked beneath a steep-sided bush reserve with a grassy flat.

→ From end of Cliff Dr, Kiama Downs, take footpath through locked gate. After

90m turn L down to beach. 0

-34.6493, 150.8597

130 PHEASANT POINT BATHS

Walk: 5 mins, 250m, easy
Facilities: Wheelchair access

ⓘ A 50m, concrete pool lacking character but set in a nice, quiet location.

→ From N end of Shoalhaven St, Kiama, walk to far end of sports field. Kiama Station 500m.

-34.6680, 150.8575

131 COALCLIFF ROCK POOL

Facilities: Toilets, shower, playground
Walk-in: 2 min, 100m, easy

ⓘ Here location is everything! This 25m, tropical-blue lap pool with kiddie pool may be unremarkable, but it's nestled at the bottom of the Illawarra escarpment, and has fantastic views around the coastline to Royal National Park.

→ Via park off Paterson Rd, Coalcliff. Coalcliff Station 850m.

-34.2464, 150.9772

140 South Booderee, Whiting Beach

South Coast

The beaches here lay claim to having the whitest sand in the world, and set against the area's impossibly clear water they certainly dazzle!

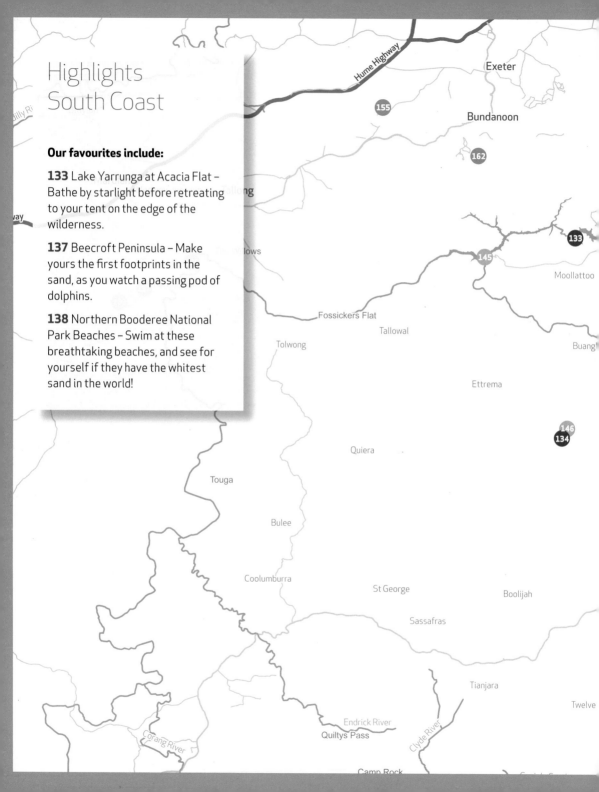

Highlights
South Coast

Our favourites include:

133 Lake Yarrunga at Acacia Flat – Bathe by starlight before retreating to your tent on the edge of the wilderness.

137 Beecroft Peninsula – Make yours the first footprints in the sand, as you watch a passing pod of dolphins.

138 Northern Booderee National Park Beaches – Swim at these breathtaking beaches, and see for yourself if they have the whitest sand in the world!

Hume Highway

Exeter

Bundanoon

155

162

133

145

Moollattoo

Fossickers Flat

Tallowal

Buang

Tolwong

Ettrema

Quiera

146
134

Touga

Bulee

Coolumburra

St George

Boolijah

Sassafras

Tianjara

Twelve

Corang River

Endrick River

Quiltys Pass

Clyde River

Camp Rock

Danjera Dam

Acacia Flat

The South Coast starts near the coastal town of Kiama and extends down past Jervis Bay. You'll find it impossible to ignore the siren song of its beautiful coastline, which meanders south for over 100km. The area also takes in the beautiful Kangaroo Valley, whose vibrant green meadows rest between the coast and the upland slopes of the Southern Highlands.

Flatrock Pool. It's easy to see why this pool, set on the edge of Budderoo National Park, is busy with locals – even midweek. It's an inviting spot and you can drive right here!

The drive up through the farmland and lush bush of Upper Kangaroo Valley is wonderfully scenic. Once here, it's obvious how the pool got its name – a large spread of flat rock spans the river, forming a natural ford crossing. A thin film of water covers the rock, spilling water from the pool into a shallower one downriver.

Lake Yarrunga at Acacia Flat. Here it's just you and the boundless water and sky. With a pervading quietude and just a few passing canoeists, this is a wonderful place to get away from it all. Lake Yarrunga sits within Morton National Park, and it's amazing that a relatively short walk brings you somewhere so remote. It's the only Sydney Catchment Authority reservoir where you're allowed to swim, and there's certainly more than enough space for it! It's such a pretty setting, though, that you'll probably be just as content to spend the day leisurely wading in and out of the water.

The gently sloping, grassy campsite juts out into the vast expanse of still lake and there's hundreds of metres of water in every direction! Shaded by tall gums, and yes, acacias, which bloom with frothy yellow flowers in spring, it's a fantastic spot for a quiet weekend.

Danjera Dam. Surrounded by bush and with a lovely feeling of isolation, it's amazing that you can drive right here! Bring your tent and spend a few easy days swimming on the threshold of a vast wilderness. This dam was created in 1972 when the valley was flooded, submerging the little mining town of Yalwal. Quivering reeds full of waterfowl edge the water – it's so natural-looking that it's easy to forget you're swimming in a reservoir.

Currarong Rock Channels. There really is nowhere else like this – two narrow, straight, interconnecting channels that run for an impressive 100m, adjacent to the shore. They're

132 Flat Rock Pool

132 FLATROCK POOL

Seclusion: Busy-average
Walk-in: 2 mins, 100m, easy

ⓘ Flatrock's popularity makes it feel a bit like a municipal pool, but one where the water is verdant. Lumpy tadpoles attach themselves to stationary limbs, and willowy gums form the changing rooms. Locals lay out picnics across the smooth, rutted rock and tethered dogs yip excitedly.

➜ From Moss Vale Rd, Barrengarry, drive 14km along Upper Kangaroo River Rd to Upper Kangaroo Valley, and park in lay-by on R before concrete ford. Flatrock Pool is below the ford on the L.

-34.6515, 150.6038

133 LAKE YARRUNGA AT ACACIA FLAT

Facilities: Toilet, campground
Seclusion: Average-secluded
Navigation: Easy
Descent: 120m
Walk-in: 30 mins, 1.65km, moderate

➜ From Moss Vale Rd, Kangaroo Valley, take Bendeela Rd W. After 3.7km continue straight onto Jacks Corner Rd. After 9.6km road becomes unsealed. After 11km enter Morton National Park at sharp L-hand corner. After 12.5km pass "Unsuitable for 2wd vehicles" sign. In dry weather 2WD access is OK. After 16.5km park on the L, beside the junction of a L turn-off on a R-hand bend in the firetrail. If you reach Beehive Point at the end of the trail, you've gone 1km too far. Walk down fire trail. After 170m you pass through a locked gate. The trail undulates before arriving at a clearing after 1.48km and then the lake and main campground soon after.

-34.7531, 150.3952 🏊 🚫 ⛺

134 DANJERA DAM

Facilities: Toilets, wood BBQs, campground
Seclusion: Busy-average
Walk-in: 1 min, 10m, easy

ⓘ It's a popular spot for canoeists and families, and there are two free, vehicle-based campgrounds to make use of – a large grassy one that runs down to the water's edge, and a smaller one from which you can explore a series of interconnecting pools below the dam slipway.

➜ From Albatross Rd, Nowra, turn off onto Yalwal Rd. After 10.1km keep L to stay on unsealed Yalwal Rd. After 24.7km you pass the Morton National Park Toorooroo Campground, then shortly after cross Yarramunmun Creek. After 25km pass through small campground. 200m further on, bear R at fork. Arrive Danjera Dam 25.8km.

-34.9223, 150.3840 🏊 ⛺ 🛶

Wilsons Beach

seemingly purpose-built for swimming, but save for a handrail and steps, are completely natural!

The water is achingly crisp aqua, with excellent visibility so you can take in all the underwater action. It's very calm, as the channels are protected on all sides and small fish seek refuge here. Tiny black-and-white striped ones hang in the water like stars, and bloated toadfish with bulging, inquisitive eyes putter along just below the surface. The adjacent grassy flat with trees and picnic tables make it a great place to spend the day.

Wilsons Beach. Dream of a little, protected cove, and Wilsons is that place! People come here for that Robinson Crusoe feeling, and you will feel duly triumphant if you chance upon it empty.

Beecroft Peninsula. The weapons range on Beecroft Peninsula has to be one of the world's most picturesque ammunition detonation sites. It has some of the most beautiful beaches and coves of Jervis Bay, and entry is free!

Long Beach is one of the very best swim spots featured in this book. It's a beautiful and protected place for a dip, with a salt-in-your-hair, sand-between-your-toes kind of feeling that makes it easy to shake off the city.

▶

135 Currarong Rock Channels

Wilsons Beach

Long Beach

136 Wilsons Beach

Low dunes and bush back the southwest-facing beach and there are far-reaching views, with the closest point, Vincentia, almost 9km away! The water is that unbelievable shade of turquoise that makes you want to strip off your clothes and dash right in, and the sand is shocking white. The beach tapers gradually for children and paddlers, and those hankering for a long swim can hug the coastline for its length. Incredibly, it's relatively little visited, so you may well have the whole gorgeous 1.8km to yourself!

A little to the north is **Cabbage Tree Beach**, another safe swimming option. It's similar to Long Beach, though south-facing, and not as pretty.

A couple of kilometres to the south is **Honeymoon Bay**, a 90m-wide, west-facing, wineglass-shaped bay. It's the stuff of postcards, and the constricted entrance means that the crystalline water is probably calmer than you'll find in your bathtub! Despite being called Honeymoon Bay, this isn't the place for a quiet romantic getaway – but for a family holiday it can't be beaten. The basic campground, which hides in the bush behind the beach, is extremely popular, and rather than the twittering of birds the predominant sound is the joyful

Honeymoon Bay

135 CURRARONG ROCK CHANNELS

Facilities: Toilets, showers, picnic tables
Seclusion: Busy-average
Walk-in: 5 mins, 300m, easy

ⓘ On their eastern end, the channels abut northwest-facing Abraham's Bosom Beach – a name given by seafaring captains who recognised its safe waters. The sheltered water is shallow for at least 50m off the beach, and it's very busy with young families.

➜ From car park off junction of Beecroft Pde and Tomerong St, Currarong, take path at 10 o'clock for 300m. 🅿 350m.

-35.0113, 150.8249 🏊 ⛵

136 WILSONS BEACH

Seclusion: Average
Navigation: Easy
Walk-in: 25 mins, 1.1km, easy

ⓘ This tiny rocky inlet has a wild and untouched feeling and, considering how close it is to the open ocean, it's incredibly sheltered. The northwest-facing beach is edged by rough, pock-marked slabs and the piercing aqua

water forms a striking contrast with the dark blue of the ocean. The visibility is fantastic and there's a lot to see under the surface. Tiny black-and-white striped fish with neon yellow dorsal fins are literally everywhere, and it's a job not to inhale any as you dive down to the sandy floor.

➜ From car park at end of Beecroft Pde, Currarong, take the bridge over the creek in the far R corner. After 250m you reach a map and a three-way split. Bear L on Wreck Walk. After 600m turn L signed Honeysuckle Point. At T-junction after 1.5km turn L again signed Honeysuckle Point, soon arriving at the beach. 🅿 600m.

-35.0038, 150.8340 🏊 ⛵

137 BEECROFT PENINSULA

ⓘ Open only to the public when not in use by the Department of Defence (usually Friday to Sunday evening), and during public and NSW school holidays. Camping fees apply and booking required – contact 02 4448 3411.

➜ Turn right onto Lighthouse Rd,

Currarong, just before reaching the town. You will then reach the Beecroft Weapons Range 24-hour manned security gate. The friendly guard will take your name, car reg number, ask where you plan to visit and give you a map. The roads are unsealed, but well signed.

Long Beach

Seclusion: Secluded
Walk-in: 2 mins, 150m. easy

➜ Via Long Beach North car park, which is 4.5km from the entrance gate.

-35.0273, 150.7794 🏖 🚫 ⛵

Cabbage Tree Beach

Seclusion: Average
Walk-in: 2 mins, 100m, easy

➜ Via Cabbage Tree Beach car park, which is 4.5km from the entrance gate.

-35.0219, 150.7726 🏖 ⛵

Honeymoon Bay

Seclusion: Busy
Walk-in: 5 mins, 250m, easy

➜ Via Honeymoon Bay day visitors car park, 6.2km from the entrance gate.

-35.0570, 150.7766 🏊 ⛺ ⛵

138 North Booderee, Iluka Beach

138 North Booderee, Bristol Point

138 North Booderee, Iluka Beach

138 North Booderee

138 North Booderee, Scottish Rocks

139 Swan Lake

warbling of children. There really is something for the whole family, with gradually shelving sand, great snorkelling, low jump rocks and interesting headlands to explore.

Northern Booderee National Park Beaches. Such is its renown, that at the mere mention of Jervis Bay, people glaze over, transported to a happy place. And with such beautiful beaches, it's little surprise! If you want yours to be the first footprints on the sand, or you want to experience the delights of these beaches without other visitors, you may need to have a sunrise or sunset dip. At these times the light becomes warm and golden, and the tranquillity of Booderee National Park is enlarged.

The busiest and most visited of all the Booderee beaches is **Green Patch Beach**. This 2km continuous stretch of north-facing sand is divided roughly in half by name only – Green Patch being the southern end. The beach is undeniably picturesque, although after rain the water can get a little murky due to overflow from a nearby creek. The big attraction, however, is the fully equipped campground. It's so popular that during school holidays, campsites are allocated via a lottery system!

▶

138 North Booderee, Iluka Beach

138 NORTHERN BOODEREE NATIONAL PARK BEACHES

→ From Jervis Bay Rd, Booderee National Park. Vehicle entry fees apply and permits are valid for 48 hours (NSW NP annual passes are not valid).

Greenpatch Beach
Facilities: Toilets, hot showers, campfires, BBQs, walk-in & car-based campground
Seclusion: Busy
Walk-in: 5 mins, 250m, easy
→ Turn L 4.5km from park entrance and follow signs to Green Patch car park.
-35.1363, 150.7238 🏖️ 🐟 ⛺

Iluka Beach
Facilities: Toilets, picnic tables
Seclusion: Average
Walk-in: 2 mins, 150m, easy
→ Turn L 4.5km from park entrance and follow signs to Iluka car park.
-35.1333, 150.7171 🏖️ 🐟

Bristol Point
Facilities: Toilets, hot showers, campfires, BBQs, campground
Seclusion: Busy-average
Walk-in: 5 mins, 240m, easy
→ Turn L 5.3km from park entrance and continue to car park. Follow signs from car park info sign to Green Patch via rock platform. Track descends to beach.
-35.1353, 150.7276 🐟 ⛰️

Scottish Rocks
Seclusion: Average-secluded
Walk-in: 5 mins, 300m, easy
→ Via lay-by on L, 6.1km from park entrance. Track descends through bush to beach.
-35.1372, 150.7391 🏖️ 🚫 🐟 🏖️

Hole in the Wall Beach
Seclusion: Average-secluded
Walk-in: 10m, 400m, easy
→ Via lay-by on L, 7km from park entrance. Track descends through bush to beach.
-35.1354, 150.7473 🏖️ 🚫 🐟 🏖️

Murray's Beach
Facilities: Toilets, picnic tables
Seclusion: Busy
Walk-in: 2 mins, 150m, easy
→ From car park at end, 8.5km from park

entrance, take track beside info sign through bush to beach.
-35.1250, 150.7578 🐟 🏖️ 🏖️

139 SWAN LAKE
Seclusion: Average
Walk-in: 1 min, 20m, easy

ⓘ In the full light of day the water is an intense lime colour, and as you dive under you're suddenly jolted into the world of technicolour. By the time the sun waves goodbye, however, the water turns peach and its glassy surface becomes yet more still. The elegant necks of swans arch in silhouette as they quietly glide across the lake and then take flight, and the night-time sounds of frogs begin. This is when Swan Lake comes into its own and really turns on the beauty!

→ Via end of partly unsealed Medlyn Ave, Sussex Inlet.
-35.1759, 150.5685 🏖️ 🐟 🚣

138 North Booderee, Murray's Beach

Green Patch continues north, becoming **Iluka Beach**. Although indistinguishable in many ways from its more famous neighbour, Iluka is much less crowded and the water is astonishingly clear. So if you don't need the facilities, this is a better destination.

Who ever said size matters? OK, so the beach at **Bristol Point** is small, but it's still one of the nicest in the whole dazzling region, and in quieter periods you could do little better than to pick this as your destination!

The calm water is very deep and spectacularly clear – it implores you to tear off your clothes and leap in. The northeast-facing beach becomes very thin at high tide, but the rock platforms that bookend it have lots of inlets with beaded weeds to snorkel around, and tiny rock pools for kids to explore. It's also just a short walk from a nice bush campground.

The water at **Scottish Rocks** is lovely and clear, and offers the full Jervis Bay sparkle on a sunny day. The north-facing beach is thin and almost disappears at high tide, but as it's one of the least visited of these beaches, it's a good place to escape the crowds.

It can come as a tough break being a beach in Booderee National Park – with so many coquettish beauties to compete with, it can be difficult to get noticed! Northwest-facing **Hole in the Wall Beach** isn't as picturesque as nearby Murray's – its ribbon of sand almost vanishes at high tide, and a small creek running into it reduces the water clarity. But even in this beach-blessed national park it rates a mention as one of the least visited.

Just inside the mouth of the bay, more diminutive **Murray's Beach** is sheltered by wildlife haven Bowen Island, which gives it some of the calmest and most protected water in the area.

Murray's is perhaps the most famous beach in the park – it's breathtakingly pretty! Luckily it's at the end of the road, and without so many enticements closer to the entry gates, it would surely be even busier. The crowds do diminish some of the serenity, but nevertheless it's an idyllic spot.

The north-facing beach is outrageously white and the aqua water glitters. It's literally mind-boggling to think that the government planned to build Australia's first nuclear power plant here. The enormous level car park is not the work of NPWS, but rather the intended site of the power plant. ▶

140 South Booderee, Kittys Beach

Thankfully the project didn't go ahead, leaving Australia still without a nuclear power plant and this stunning beach untouched.

Swan Lake is a tranquil and truly magical spot. Poetically named, the heart-shaped lake is something totally different to the endless sandy beaches of Jervis Bay. There really are swans here, and it's completely overlooked by tourists!

The lake is backed by bush and a thin ribbon of beach that tapers gradually into the water. It's decorously calm, and as it's brackish you're guaranteed no sharks. So strike out for the horizon with freedom – although you're unlikely to get there as it's over 2.5km away!

Southern Booderee National Park Beaches. Comparatively few people ever venture to the ocean side of Booderee National Park, but those that make the effort are well rewarded. The water here is at least as stunning a hue as Jervis Bay's more famous beaches, yet you actually run the chance of having it to yourself – a feat pretty much unheard of if you stick to the well-trodden tourist traps! This walk through the bush takes in three spectacular swimming spots.

140 South Booderee, Whiting Beach

Maybe you've been to the Caribbean, or seen the glacial lakes in New Zealand; for sure you've noticed how intensely blue the water can be in your local municipal pool. Well, it's like that at **Whiting Beach**. A protected, 350m-long bay full of the most obscenely milky-blue water. You'll want to swim here. In fact, we challenge you not too!

But why stop at one swim when you can continue on and swim at two more delightful, out of the way locations?

140 South Booderee, Black's Harbour

140 SOUTHERN BOODEREE BEACHES

Seclusion: Average-secluded
Orientation: Southwest-facing, except northwest-facing Kitty's Beach
Navigation: Moderate
Descent: 150m
Walk-in: 110 mins, 5.5km, easy-moderate

➜ Turn L off Wreck Bay Rd, Jervis Bay Territory (vehicle entry fees apply and permits are valid for 48 hours – NSW NP annual passes are not valid), onto unsealed Stony Creek Rd, and continue for 2km to Steamers Bay car park. The walk starts at the gated fire trail signed Steamers Beach. Ignore turning L after 60m. After 1.3km follow signs to Blacks Waterhole. After 2.6km continue past Blacks Waterhole, where swimming is not permitted. At a T-junction after 3km (just past Blacks Waterhole) turn L to Whiting Beach. After 3.5km arrive at Whiting Headland turn off R. A 200m path leads to a rock ledge at the bay's edge.

ⓘ **Whiting Beach.** It's tricky to recommend the best time to visit. At low tide a sandy beach appears, although with shallower water, the bay doesn't look quite so spectacular. At high tide access to the water can be difficult – you have to wade to the beach (a narrow strip of seaweedy sand) from the rock platform or dive in over oystery rocks. But, once you're in…!

➜ Return back up to main track. Turn R. Ignore one vehicle track on R. After 500m turn off R to Blacks Harbour – it is 200m down.

-35.1773, 150.6957 🏊

ⓘ **Black's Harbour** is a little-visited, narrow, 200m-long channel, cleft between a breakwater populated by soporific cormorants on one side, and a rocky headland. The contrast of the sandstone breakwater and the blush granite headland with the absinthe-coloured water is striking, and it's easy to feel you've arrived someplace special. Despite being on the ocean side of Jervis Bay, Blacks Harbour is protected in most weathers. The water is fantastically deep, dropping to 3–4m and even then the visibility remains flawless! It teems with aquatic life, and as you swim microscopic fish surround you like a cloud of glitter. Although there's no real beach to speak of

the rock ledges provide easy access into the water and are good to camp out on.

➜ Return back up to main track. Turn R. After 30m turn R to Kittys Beach. After 625m with the beach below turn R. Arrive 750m. Around low tide there is an optional return to Black's Harbour via the rock shelf and a small, sheltered unnamed beach with interesting water life.

-35.1841, 150.6946 🏖

ⓘ **Kittys Beach** is small and tucked away, and given that it's one of the most remote beaches in the area, it has a magical hidden feeling. People seem to come here to get away from it all, so even if you don't have it all to yourself, you're assured of having a quiet time. The beach is protected, and even on a blustery day its waves are only tiny. In the water you pass over stingray after stingray hunkered down in the sand, two eyes protruding watchfully, and as you hover over them they rise up and flutter like aquatic crepes before gracefully zooming into the blue. A few beach side trees provide pleasant shady areas under which to rest.

-35.1902, 150.6955 🏊

And if you have time...

141 WERRI BEACH ROCK POOL

Facilities: Toilets, change-rooms
Walk-in: 2 mins, 100m, easy

ⓘ A 23m-long concrete pool with kiddie pool, cut into a vast intertidal shelf, with views across to the pretty rolling hills of Kiama.

→ Via car park at S end of Pacific Ave, Gerringong. 🚗 500m.

-34.7440, 150.8360 📧

142 GERRINGONG BOAT HARBOUR ROCK POOL

Facilities: Toilets, picnic tables, BBQs
Walk-in: 2 mins, 165m, easy

ⓘ A 35m pool in a quiet, cliffside location. It has a concrete beach with tiered ledges – although they miss out on the afternoon sunshine.

→ From car park at end of Jupiter St, Gerringong, walk N. 🚗 850m.

-34.7497, 150.8332

143 HAMPDEN BRIDGE POOL

Facilities: Toilets
Walk-in: 1 min, 50m, easy

ⓘ A long pool set under the historic bridge in Kangaroo Valley. Traffic noise and litter prevent it being a destination, but if you're passing it's a convenient place to cool off.

→ Via car park off Moss Vale Rd, Kangaroo Valley, on the village side of Hampden Bridge. 🚗 50m.

-34.7275, 150.5211

144 BENDEELA CAMPGROUND

Facilities: Toilets, campground
Walk-in: 1 min, 50m, easy

ⓘ A vast, free, vehicle-based campground, fronting 1.5km of the Kangaroo River arm of Lake Yarrunga. It's always popular with families, and is a good place for swimming, as well as launching a canoe. If you like wombats, there always seems to be one about.

→ From Moss Vale Rd, Kangaroo Valley, take Bendeela Rd W. (NB road turns L). Arrive 6km.

-34.7393, 150.4703 📧 🍴 ⛺

145 LAKE YARRUNGA AT TALLOWA DAM

Facilities: Toilets, picnic tables, BBQs
Walk-in: 1 min, 40m, easy

ⓘ It's a long way down the road from Kangaroo Valley to this dam, but it's a good place if you like being unbounded in your swimming.

→ Via car park at end of Tallowa Dam Rd, Moollattoo.

-34.7697, 150.3159 📧

146 YALWAL CREEK AT TOOROOROO

Facilities: Toilets, picnic tables, BBQs, campground
Walk-in: 5 mins, 350m, easy

ⓘ A sleepy, little-visited pool close to a small, free, vehicle-based campground in Morton National Park.

→ From Albatross Rd, Nowra, turn onto Yalwal Rd. After 10km keep L to stay on unsealed Yalwal Rd. After 24.7km turn R signed Morton National Park, Toorooroo (if you reach Yarramunmun Creek you've gone 100m too far). The road splits immediately. Turn L to picnic area and take path from the

150 Greenfields Beach

Secret Beach

far L corner. Descend steps at 285m bear L signed Yalwal Creek Access, to pool.
-34.9145, 150.3885 ⛰

147 HARES BEACH

Facilities: Toilet, picnic tables
Walk-in: 2 mins, 125m, easy
ⓘ A classically beautiful, 2.5km long, Jervis Bay beach, backed by national park, with white as white, squeaky sand and clear aqua water. It's free to visit, but gets few visitors. It's an idyllic spot if you can cope with the seemingly ever present, ravenous horse-flies!

→ Near Callala Bay, drive E along Currarong Rd for 2.6km from Coonemia Rd junction, towards Currarong. Turn R onto fire trail signed Red Point. Continue 2.2km to car park, then take path beside info sign through picnic area. 🅿 700m.
-34.9911, 150.7508 🏊

148 HUSKISSON SEA POOL

Facilities: Toilets, playground
Walk-in: 1 min, 50m, easy
ⓘ 50m concrete, fenced pool, kiddie pool

→ Via car park at E end of Owen St, Huskisson. 🅿 220m.
-35.0378, 150.6726 🏊

149 SECRET BEACH

Walk-in: 10 mins, 420m, easy
ⓘ It isn't marked on the tourist maps and council signs mark Nelsons Beach to the north and Blenheim to the south, with Secret Beach remaining, well – secret! The little, east-facing pocket of sand has sloping rock shelves either side. It would be crowded if there were other people here, but if there isn't, it could be just what you're after!

→ From car park at N end of Frederick St,Vincentia, take track N, which runs parallel to water, ignoring L turns. Follow for 320m before taking steps R down to Nelsons Beach. Walk R around the rocky headland to Secret Beach. 🅿 750m.
-35.0801, 150.6922 🚻

150 GREENFIELDS BEACH

Facilities: Toilets, shower, BBQs
Walk-in: 1 min, 50m, easy

ⓘ By far the most picturesque beach on the south side of Jervis Bay, not in Booderee National Park. Surrounded by bush, with hallmark aqua water, powdery white sand, and sweeping views – this east-facing beach is justly popular.

→ Via car park at S end of Elizabeth Dr, Vincentia. 🅿 730m.
-35.0878, 150.6925 🚻 🏖

151 ST GEORGES BASIN AT PALM BEACH

Facilities: Toilets, picnic tables, BBQs
Walk-in: 1 min, 20m, easy
ⓘ The vibe here is more laidback than at nearby beaches – more round-shouldered grandmas in one-pieces than tanned French tourists in bikinis. It's not spectacular, but the quiet setting has expansive bush views. The brackish water of this huge inland lagoon is very clear and calm, and the infinitesimally sloping sand is perfect anyone a little wobbly on their feet.

→ Via car park off Greville Ave, Sanctuary Point (at Sanctuary Point Rd).
-35.1157, 150.6355 q

Mermaids Pool

Southern
Highlands

The cultivated charm of the quaint townships, rolling farmland and vineyards for which this area is known gives way to bush of dramatic and rugged beauty which abounds with memorable places to swim.

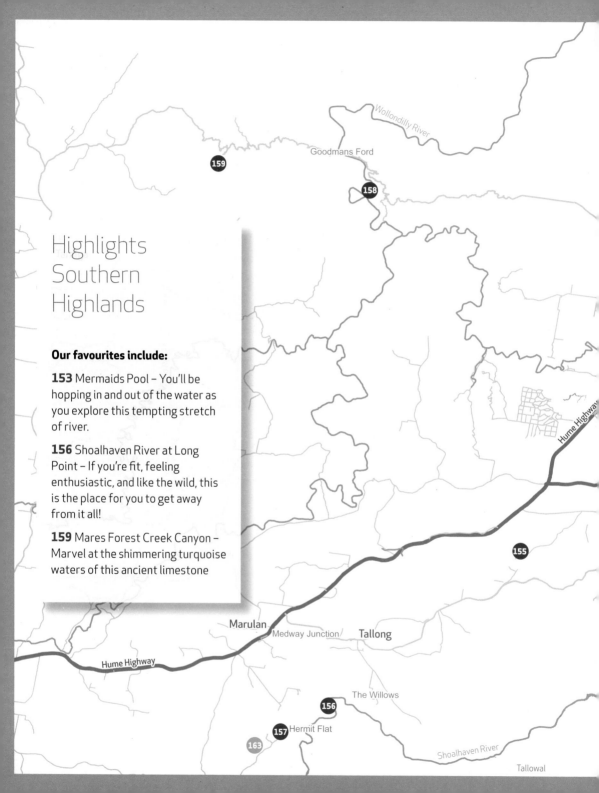

Highlights
Southern
Highlands

Our favourites include:

153 Mermaids Pool – You'll be hopping in and out of the water as you explore this tempting stretch of river.

156 Shoalhaven River at Long Point – If you're fit, feeling enthusiastic, and like the wild, this is the place for you to get away from it all!

159 Mares Forest Creek Canyon – Marvel at the shimmering turquoise waters of this ancient limestone

Wollondilly River

Goodmans Ford

Hume Highway

Marulan

Medway Junction

Tallong

The Willows

Hermit Flat

Shoalhaven River

Tallowal

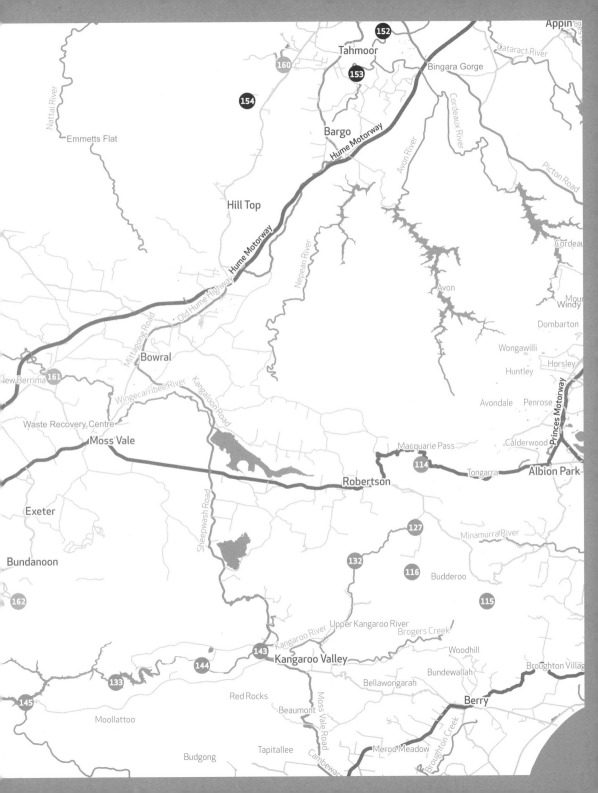

152 Maldon Weir

153 Maldon Weir

The Southern Highlands rise over 900m above sea level. It's not just cream teas, antique shops and wine tastings; here you'll find landscapes as dramatic as anywhere, as well as some exceptionally good and little-known swimming spots. There's a wonderful diversity for the wild swimmer – so what are you waiting for?

Maldon Weir. The Nepean River here is blocked up by a high weir, and revellers come to zoom down its steeply curving concrete slope on plastic bread trays, before tumbling into the pool below. It's not just for thrill-seekers though, as the weir also creates a deep infinity pool upriver which extends for over 2km – surely long enough for anyone?

Such is the split nature of the place that your experience could vary drastically, depending on the timing of your visit. Access to the main pool is limited, so it can quickly feel crowded – shrinking its tranquillity. The weir is popular with local youths, and the lovely bush setting is marred by graffiti and rubbish. If this doesn't faze you, you're in luck, because this place is just a short detour off the Hume Highway, and makes a fun side-trip.

Mermaids Pool is the promoted draw card of the beautiful Bargo River, and its image features in tourist brochures. While the pool is a destination in itself, the whole river here is an explorer's paradise, and it's wonderful to while away a day discovering its swimming delights.

The pool is gasp-worthy on first sight, and looks unmistakably Australian. It sits at the base of a colossal amphitheatre with dramatic, sheer walls. It's a humbling experience to swim in its dark green water, as the cliffs and trees and sky climb on forever around you. The water is unfathomably deep and there's a rope swing to take you zooming out over the pool. For the reckless, there's also a rumbling waterfall to jump from. Sadly, there's the usual graffiti and rubbish that seem to accompany well-known pools, but nevertheless it remains a first-class place for wild swimming.

Before you arrive at Mermaids you'll pass **See Through Pool** – a pool with a curious, submerged pot-hole pool in its centre. The river also has numerous other pools that are never far from the track. So why not embark on a swimming odyssey and sample them all?

Little River Pools. If you fancy spending a fun day pool-hopping, this is worth the journey. The pools don't have the wow factor of some others in the area, but they do have an ▶

153 Mermaids Pool

152 MALDON WEIR

Seclusion: Busy-average
Navigation: Easy
Descent: 25m
Walk-in: 5 mins, 300m, moderate
➜ Via end of Wilton Park Rd, Wilton. Walk through locked gate and continue along road. After 300m, with the weir directly below, climb over crash barrier and scramble down the rough path to river. If the weir is too busy for your liking it's possible to walk 200m downriver to a quieter pool below an old bridge.

-34.2037, 150.6301 🪧🍴

153 MERMAIDS POOL

Seclusion: Busy-average
Navigation: Moderate
Descent: 40m
Walk-in: 60 mins, 2.05km, moderate
ⓘ **Caution must be taken near Mermaids Pool. The dangerous location makes it unsuitable for children.**

➜ Via car park at N end of Charlies Point Rd, Bargo, just before junction with Rockford Rd. Take path that leads underneath the bridge and continue downriver. After 900m it's necessary to leave the river's edge where there's an old red engine and climb up above the bank. After 1.15km drop back down to **See Through Pool**, which you will see below. Return to the higher path. After 1.6km drop down to Mermaids Pool. Access to water is dangerous from here; safe access can be found at the far end of the pool. To get there, cross the river and take the path that leads up the cliff on the farside. At top bear R. The path is tricky to follow, but it isn't close to the cliff top, so keep back. You need to reach some exposed cliff-top rocks about 100m after the farend of the pool, opposite sheer stratified cliffs. Walk down through a chimney in the rocks, and then bear R to the first part of a rock overhang. Descend bearing R, back towards the pool, until just above the riverbed. Continue upriver below the cliff line. There's a 2m scramble-down just before the pool. At the pool there's a jumble of boulders. It isn't possible to reach the rock ledges that flank the pool without getting wet, but a few of the boulders are large enough to sit out on.

-34.2396, 150.6070 🍴🧗📷

154 LITTLE RIVER POOLS

Seclusion: Average-secluded
Navigation: Moderate
Descent: 90m
Walk-in: 40 mins, 1.8km, moderate
➜ Via car park at W end of Boundary Rd, Buxton (note: it continues straight, but unsealed after junction with Buxton Ave). Walk back 40m and go through locked gate on R, adjacent to the end property. Keep to this fire trail, ignoring turn-offs – this runs flat before becoming steep and badly eroded. After 850m you pass through another locked gate. Just beyond this is Little River and the first pool on your R. To continue, cross over the river above the pool and turn R, downriver. After 1.24km you arrive at a large clearing next to the second pool. Continuing on, after 1.6km bear R at fork. After 1.8km the sides of the valley suddenly close in and you soon reach the final, tiny pools. It's difficult to venture any further than here. 📷 900m.

-34.2621, 150.5118 📷

155 Stingray Swamp

attractive bush setting that can be reached in just 20 minutes, *and* you're unlikely to have to share them with anyone.

The first pool you arrive at is relatively small with several rock platforms to sit out on. In the warmer months it's surrounded by wildflowers, and sprinklings of intense yellow petals float above the greenery. The bees, attracted by the pollen, sound like race-cars rounding corners at speed.

If you continue downstream you arrive at another pool with a 1.5m-high waterfall tumbling over an impressive rock ledge overhang. It's a classic waterhole and would be perfect, but for it being popular with trail bikers and showing some unfortunate signs of use.

Further on, the river becomes full of carved boulders, nestled among which is a cluster of very little-visited plunge pools.

Stingray Swamp. The word 'swamp' doesn't arouse delight in swimmers, but this pool is actually a lovely place to swim and looks like the quintessential Australian billabong.

Stingray is a medium-sized pool with a small sandy beach, surrounded by ferns and long-legged white gums. A rope swing on the far bank hangs over deep water, and there's even a ladder to help you climb out.

The pool is part of a system of highland swamps that eventually feed into the Wollondilly River and Warragamba Dam. These swamps can date back hundreds of thousands of years, and act like giant purifiers, slowly filtering water

Little River Pools

through layers of peat. During times of low rainfall the water changes from golden brown to deep red, like blood! This colour comes from the surrounding Button Grass vegetation, but the effect is truly bizarre.

There's space for a few tents, and it makes a great place for an overnighter; just off the Hume Highway it couldn't be easier to get a dose of the bush. There's Black Cockatoos and their mournful screeches, Splendid Blue Wrens as light as air, tittering in the scrub, and a whole orchestra of frogs that become ear-splitting at dusk. You might even be lucky enough to see a mob of kangaroos bound into the pool for a cooling swim. What could be more Australian than that? The tiny nearby village of Penrose has some of the friendliest locals you could hope to meet so do them a favour by taking particular care of this wonderful place.

Shoalhaven River at Long Point. This little-visited part of the Shoalhaven River nestles in a deep, deep valley, on the edge of boundless Morton National Park. It's characterised by slow-moving pools interspersed with pebble-strewn rapids, and there are two fantastic places to pitch your tent. What could be better than drying off after your last swim of the day before starting a fire and getting dinner on?

The land along this bend in the Shoalhaven was once cleared for cattle grazing but is now full of wildflowers and grazing Kangaroos. **MacCallum Flat Pool** is 250m long and bordered by a sand bank, and sheer, craggy rockface, which fills your view opposite. The sand bank is sprinkled with river oaks, but remains a sunny camping option. The water drops steeply from the bank quickly becoming deep, and it's a dramatic, wild place to swim.

Alternatively, a shorter tromp upstream leads you to **Louise Reach** – an immense 800m-long pool, 100m across. You're never going to find a river pool bigger than this! It's particularly good for languorous swims, as the water is so unhurried that it captures everything surrounding it on its mirror-like surface.

A restful grove of pencil-thin river oaks borders the pool, and perhaps makes an even more idyllic spot to camp – although it's shady, so if you're after sunshine head to MacCallum Flat.

156 Shoalhaven River at Long Point

156 Shoalhaven River at Long Point

155 Stingray Swamp

155 STINGRAY SWAMP

Seclusion: Average

Navigation: Easy

Descent: 5m

Walk-in: 5 mins, 350m, easy

➔ From Penrose Train Station, travel S on Penrose Rd. After a short distance take bridge over tracks, then immediately turn R onto Kareela Rd. After 350m this becomes unsealed Old Argyle Rd. After another 1.4km the road bends sharply to the L; turn R here (effectively straight). At a T-junction after another 200m turn L. After a further 650m keep L. Continue on this road for 900m; you will cross a small creek ford and pass farmland on your R, before taking first L. Park after 100m and take trail on R to pool.

-34.6434, 150.2276

156 SHOALHAVEN RIVER AT LONG POINT

Facilities: Campsites

Seclusion: Secluded

Descent: 500m

MacCallum Flat

Walk-in: 150 mins, 5.65km, moderate-hard

Navigation: Hard, Caoura GR 310480

-34.7749, 150.0610

Louise Reach

Walk-in: 120 mins, 4.3km, moderate-hard

Navigation: Hard, Caoura GR 303468

-34.7846, 150.0521

➔ Via the end of unsealed Long Point Rd, Tallong. McCallum's Flat Track starts at the far corner of the car park. After 170m there's a lookdown over the flat and river on the L. The track continues just under the ridgeline to a point overlooking the Marulan quarry where there's a walk registration book. Follow the track as it gently descends the ridge. After 1km you'll pass above a saddle overlooking Kingpin Mountain. The track zigzags down to the saddle before continuing on around the R-hand side of the mountain. The track then descends gently towards the river. After 2.1km the river comes back into view and the track switchbacks innumerable times. You may be able to hear the roar of Louise Rapids. After 3.8km you arrive at a flat, grassy clearing where there's an arrow post. This points towards the track on your return journey. You now have two options. **MacCallum Flat:** From the arrow post there is no path, but bear L / E, walking downriver, parallel to the Shoalhaven. Keep to the same elevation – you'll soon pass a small knoll on your R and shortly pick up a faint path that leads to the former meadow. Head to the far end of the meadow, before dropping R to the river. The water is still shallow here, so continue downriver along the pebbles and sand until the river suddenly slows down to a pool beside a large, sandy area. It's opposite a sheer, vertically layered, sandstone cliff with two distinctive holes in a recently exposed orange area. The pool is about 850m from the end of the meadow, 1.85km from arrow post. **Louise Reach:** From the arrow post turn sharp R / W. You shortly arrive beside a small creek. Turn L and walk through a small, grassy campsite, then cross the creek and walk upriver, parallel to the Shoalhaven. 300m after the crossing you arrive at a shady, grassy campsite on the riverbank next to a huge, wide stretch of river, 500m from arrow post.

Shoalhaven River at Long Point

153 See Through Pool

153 Mermaids Pool

157 Bungonia Creek

Bungonia Creek

Bungonia Creek at Slot Canyon. In a primeval, Tolkienesque landscape where boulders are as big as buses, 'large' takes on a new meaning! Limestone cliffs dwarf you as they loom from 400m above – that's a third as tall again as Centrepoint Tower! Even though your neck will hurt from all the craning, it's impossible not to look up and feel humbled by the enormity of it all.

Out of the jumble of rocks filling the canyon floor, the modestly-sized pool suddenly appears. It's a truly breathtaking experience to swim as you take in the scenery around you.

This book tries to steer clear of *bushwalks where you can swim*, and concentrates instead on *swims you need to walk to*. This pool is definitely leaning towards the former. However, it's such a spectacular walk and location, and if you're fit and enjoy both walking and swimming it;s an absolute must-visit!

Wollondilly River Nature Reserve. Warm water alert: do not swim here in summer if you prefer cold water! The river here is so slow moving that it soaks up all the warmth of the sun, and on a summer's afternoon it's easy to luxuriate in its bath-like waters.

▶

Wollondilly River Nature Reserve

157 BUNGONIA CREEK AT SLOT CANYON

Facilities: Full amenities at car-based campground near start of walk.

Seclusion: Average-secluded

Navigation: Hard, get free map from office.

Descent: 380m

Walk-in: 300 mins, 4.23km circuit, hard

ⓘ Track is subject to closure after heavy rain. Camping fees apply and bookings required – contact NPWS.

→ Via Bungonia National Park (vehicle entry fees apply) at the end of The Lookdown Rd, Bungonia. After registering your intentions at the office, park in William Mitchell car park. Note that distances for this walk are not cumulative. Follow the Red Track markers through the locked gate. At the top of the knoll the track forks R and descends over loose scree, sometimes very steeply. It descends into a gully on the L, crossing to the far side after a spring, before rejoining it nearer the canyon. Arrive at Bungonia Creek after 830m. Turn R into the canyon and follow downstream. There is no track. The cliffs tower above you on both sides. If there hasn't been much recent rain the creek may be flowing underground, leaving the bed dry. Towards the end of the canyon there's a jumble of massive boulders which you'll have to pick your way over or under. Just as the canyon widens to the pool, 800m from the start of the canyon. Continue downstream on the R-hand side. The boulders soon decrease in size, but it's slow-going and there are a few other little pools to tempt you. The Red Track exit up from the creek is 800m from the main pool – it's on the R, next to a large metal sign detailing blasting. Keep an eye out for a dip in the cliffs on the L (which is where the quarry is); it's more or less opposite. Don't forget to cool off before ascending – you will be hot soon enough – there's a long shallow pool just beyond the exit sign. Thankfully the way up is not quite as steep as the way down, but it's brutal nevertheless, and while the canyon is usually shaded, the route out is north-facing and quite exposed. The climb eases 850m from the creek. Finally at the top, after 1.2km, the track junctions with the White and Green tracks. Turn R here; it's just a gentle 600m further back to the car park.

-34.7971, 150.0195 🅰 🚶 🔲

158 WOLLONDILLY RIVER NATURE RESERVE

Facilities: Toilets, showers, campfires at car-based campground

Seclusion: Secluded

Navigation: Easy-moderate

Descent: 50m

Walk-in: 80 mins, 4.6km, easy

ⓘ The walk starts from Wollondilly River Station, where there's an excellent and popular campground, next to an enormous, campers-only river pool. Camping fees apply and booking required, see: www.wollondillyriverstation.com

→ Via Wombeyan Caves Rd, 15.5km E of Wombeyan Caves, 45.5km W of the Old Hume Hwy, Mittagong. The walk starts from the gate on the Wombeyan Caves-side of the Wollondilly River bridge

159 Mares Forest Creek Canyon

A nature reserve backs the river, but the land was, until recently, a farm and its past life is still readily apparent – the walk takes you through riverside meadows that, rather than being grazed by cows, are one of the best places around Sydney to see kangaroos. At dusk it's difficult to avoid stumbling into them; everywhere you turn there are more, noiselessly munching on long grass.

Mares Forest Creek Canyon. This swim is sure to bring out your inner adventurer. For the amphibious amongst us, it simply doesn't get any better! It's terrific to become part of the creek, half-wild yourself, as you spend a hot day swimming and rock-hopping up its 1.5km length.

As you swim through the stunning canyon, it's tough mentally catching up with your senses as you take it all in. The beautiful opalescent water shifts from milky turquoise to sparkling emerald as it flows through the white pock-marked canyon. The limestone is thought to be over 400 million years old, and the walls radiate with dancing rays of sunshine reflected up from the water.

At times the walls are barely an arm-span apart, and you hear the glub-glub of your wake disturbing the reverent solitude. Further upstream there are pools with deep sections – perfect for plunging into from the nearby rocks. The water is so clear that the fine details of the floor are all still visible from a height. Skinks and water dragons are everywhere, and from time to time dragonflies will land on you and hitch a ride upstream.

The drive to the canyon, along the largely unsealed road from Mittagong, with countless blind corners and sheer drop-offs, is spectacular if slightly nail-biting! The canyon is within the popular Wombeyan Karst Conservation Reserve, whose caves are also worth visiting.

159 Mares Forest Creek Canyon

at Goodmans Ford. Follow vehicle track upriver through the campsite. After 450m pass through a locked gate into the nature reserve. After 3.3km the track becomes Horse Flat Management Trail. You leave the river here and cross a large former meadow. After 4.1km bear R around the fenced-off farmhouse and buildings, and then L at the far end of the fence. This is then signposted River Flat Management Trail. Just after the sign the trail bends R, then 60m after take the L fork which descends to the river where there's an old concrete slab with pipe fittings.

-34.3390, 150.0952 🏊 ⛺ ↪

159 MARES FOREST CREEK CANYON

Facilities: Full amenities at car-based campground near start of walk

Seclusion: Average

Navigation: Moderate

Descent: 60m

Walk-in: 30 mins, 1.6km, moderate

ⓘ Water shoes or sandals are essential for grip and comfort. The canyon is narrow and only receives sun for a short period of the day. To experience it at its most spectacular, it's essential to be in the canyon before noon. The water is always crisp, and, as you'll be hopping in and out of it, rash vests provide welcome extra warmth even on very hot days. On cooler days a wetsuit is a must. Camping fees apply and booking required – contact NPWS.

→ Via Wombeyan Karst Conservation Reserve, Wombeyan Caves Rd (66km from Mittagong – allow up to two hours for this drive as there are large sections that are narrow, unsealed and winding). Follow signs for Mares Forest Creek Canyon from opposite the reserve's visitor centre. The walk starts across the small footbridge and gently ascends Victoria Arch, before descending to the creek, while ignoring all L turns. Once at the creek, leave anything you don't want to take with you up the canyon (there are some large boulders to stow bags and clothes under). The first pool, which has a pipe along its side, is immediately upstream on your R, and this is the start of your amphibious journey. From here it's possible to progress through the canyon for about 1.5km although the beauty of this swim is that you simply explore as far as you want before turning back. From the first pool, follow the creek upstream. You'll find a series of long, deep pools interspersed with sections of shallow water or rocks. The canyon eventually opens up and terminates at a deep pool below a waterfall. This last pool is one of the best and is great for jumping.

-34.3169, 149.9640 🍴 ⛺ ⬓

And if you have time...

160 LAKE COURIDJAH

Facilities: Toilets, picnic tables, BBQs
Walk-in: 1 min, 30m, easy

ⓘ This lake has been an important wildlife habitat for 15 million years. It was also a beautiful place to swim. However, water levels have dropped in recent years, believed to be linked to mining in the area, and it's now sadly rain-dependent.

→ From West Parade, Couridjah, just S of junction with Bargo River Rd, enter Thirlmere Lakes NP (vehicle entry fees apply) on unsealed road. After 1.1km turn L, then 100m further, turn R into Lake Couridjah car park. 🅟 1.3km.

-34.2317, 150.5436 🛈

161 WINGECARRIBEE RIVER AT BERRIMA RESERVE

Walk-in: 10 mins, 520m, easy

ⓘ The dam here makes for good swimming, irrespective of rainfall. The warm water and lack of flow mean it's perfect for lazy swims, and the pretty bush setting makes it seem surprisingly natural.

→ From end of Oldbury St, Berrima, (Oldbury St continues straight as an unsealed road on R-hand bend 500m from the Old Hume Hwy). Take fire trail ahead. After 400m turn L and continue to river. 🅟 750m.

-34.4945, 150.3424 🛈

162 BUNDANOON CREEK

Facilities: Campsite.
Navigation: Moderate
Descent: 300m
Walk-in: 50 mins, 1.4km, moderate-hard

ⓘ It's a long way down, but thankfully it's not always too steep. Once here you'll pass a few boulder-bounded, bushy pools – the last one is as private a location as you could ever wish for. Dragonflies are literally everywhere!

→ Via end of The Gullies Rd, Bundanoon. After passing through the Morton NP entrance (vehicle entry fees apply), continue along the one-way loop road for 2.1km to the Tooths Lookout car park. Take the track to the left of the car park, signed Tooths Lookout Cliff Climb Track to Bundanoon Creek. After 150m you arrive at Tooths Lookout over Bundanoon Creek Gorge. The track descends steeply with steps at first, but then becomes more moderate. After 560m turn R at fork to Bundanoon Creek. Arrive at the creek after 1.2km. The end of the pool at which you arrive is a bit weedy, so cross over the boulders and turn L, upstream. There is room for one tent beside the pool, 50m up from the crossing, and another a further 100m upstream. By walking below the cliffs you'll pass another pool and the final pool 200m from the crossing. 🚉 Bundanoon Station 3.6km.

-34.6842, 150.3102 ⛺

163 BUNGONIA CREEK AT YELLOW TRACK

Navigation: Moderate
Descent: 60m
Walk-in: 20 mins, 700m, moderate

162 Bundanoon Creek

168 Bungonia Creek at Yellow Track

ⓘ If a stroll to the lookdowns is enough to quench your thirst for adventure, or if you've already been down to Slot Canyon and want another day away from Sydney, but a rather less strenuous one, this is a great place to head! The scenery isn't as dramatic, but getting here is a relative cinch. Here the creek tumbles through a series of narrow, cascading waterfalls into a pool of caramel water. Although you won't find a lot of shade, there are countless slabs to dry off on.

→ Via Bungonia National Park (vehicle entry fees apply) at the end of The Lookdown Rd, Bungonia. After registering your intentions at the office, park just before the water tanks on the camping area loop. The walk is signed with yellow markers (track subject to closure after heavy rain). After 175m the Yellow Track forks L and descends to Bungonia Creek. Take note of the markers for your return, then turn R downstream and rock-hop 280m to pool.

-34.8088, 149.9971 🔺🎒

161 Wingecarribee River

165 Minerva Pool

Sydney West

While not large in number, the swimming spots that do exist here are big in size!

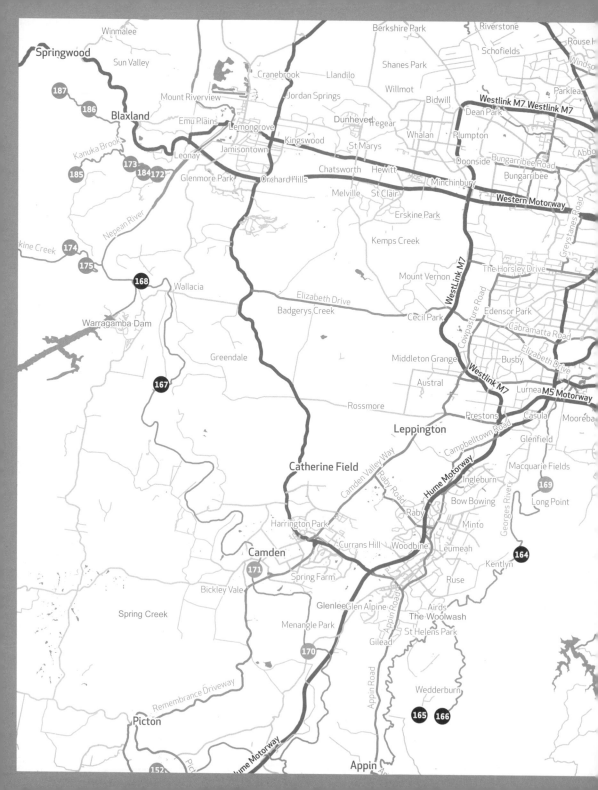

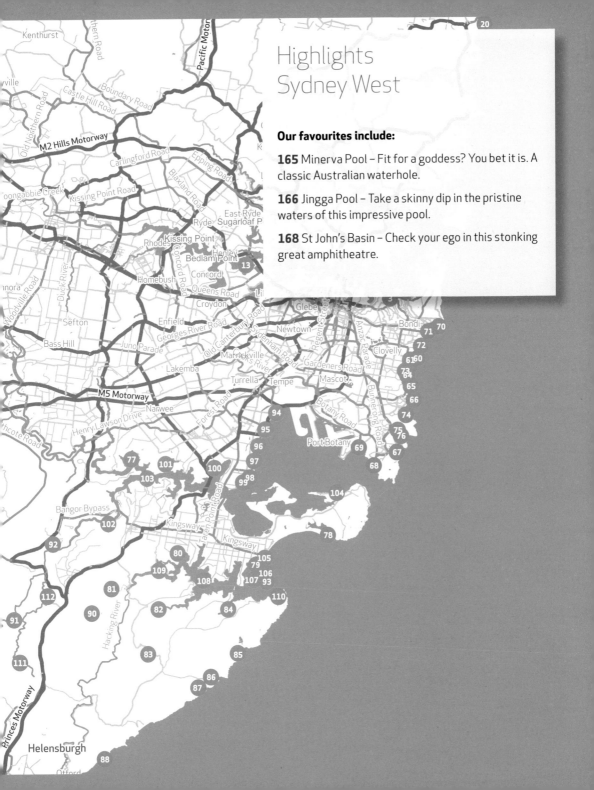

Highlights
Sydney West

Our favourites include:

165 Minerva Pool – Fit for a goddess? You bet it is. A classic Australian waterhole.

166 Jingga Pool – Take a skinny dip in the pristine waters of this impressive pool.

168 St John's Basin – Check your ego in this stonking great amphitheatre.

166 Jingga Pool

164 The Basin

Most people only ever view Western Sydney from a car hurtling along the motorway. Yet amid its sprawling suburbs and farmland there are unexpected pockets of bush, surrounding impressive basins and waterholes.

The Basin, Kentlyn. Don't be put off by the random scrawlings of graffiti, the empty cans and solitary, forgotten thongs that litter the end of Georges River Road. Once you descend into the valley, the bush opens up to reveal The Basin and you're in a whole other world!

The Basin is a whacking great waterhole, popular with local youths on weekends. Despite this popularity, it doesn't seem to have the litter problem of other hotspots.

If you still want more, you can take a side trip to a beautiful downstream section of Georges River. The water here is startlingly still, and the tall gums covering the narrow, rocky valley mirror their ghostly trunks on its surface. The feeling is different than that at The Basin, and it's a picturesque and much less-visited spot for a swim.

Minerva Pool. In the relatively little-visited Dharawal National Park, this classic Australian waterhole is certainly worthy of a goddess! When you step down from the bush track and see it, you really feel like you've found somewhere special.

Jingga Pool. When the sign says that the path to this pool is steep, it's not kidding! This walk is certainly more taxing ▶

165 Minerva Pool

164 THE BASIN, KENTLYN

Seclusion: Busy-average
Navigation: Moderate
Descent: 80m
Walk-in: 20 mins, 1km, easy-moderate

ⓘ The water is a beautiful tannin-brown, and descends into The Basin in a bubbling curtain from a curving ledge. This large ledge provides lots of space to be warmed by the sun alongside the resident skinks. Just beyond the falls, the water drops off steeply and becomes very deep.

➜ Via car park at N end of Georges River Rd, Kentlyn. For The Basin, take track from car park R at 3 o'clock. It's marked by metal posts, but they no longer have direction markers on them. After 90m bear L at fork. After 190m bear R at fork. The track runs fairly level for 620m then descends with well-made steps to the basin.

For **Georges River** below The Basin, take the fire trail from the car park that runs flat and straight behind the locked gate. After 450m it turns sharp

R. The trail then descends gently to the river and a long pool. Cross over the river on the stepping-stones, and walk upstream for 50m to a small sandbank and flat rock. Arrive 20 mins, 1.4km.

-34.0490, 150.8943 🖼

165 MINERVA POOL

Seclusion: Average
Navigation: Moderate
Descent: 80m
Walk-in: 30 mins, 1.5km, easy-moderate

ⓘ The pool is a near perfect 40m oval, enclosed by a horseshoe-shaped rock platform, with a huge monolithic boulder standing like a sentinel opposite. The water is clean and deep, and good for jumping into. A waterfall gushes assuredly, even in times of drought, because of hanging swamps upstream in the park.

➜ From car park at end of Victoria Rd, Wedderburn, walk through gate into Dharawaral National Park and continue along sealed road. After 200m turn R on 10T Management Trail. Ignore turnings. After 800m you reach a T-junction. Turn

L, and then after another 75m turn R onto a path, which leads directly to the pool.

-34.1628, 150.8211 🍴

164 The Basin

Jingga Pool

St John's Basin

Norton's Basin

than the one to nearby Minerva Pool; however, the flip side is that it receives even fewer visitors.

Jingga means "nice and sweet" in the Dharawal language, and while this may be an appropriate reference to the taste of the water, the pool itself has too strong a presence to be deemed merely nice and sweet. It's a magical place to swim, and as you're unlikely to be interrupted, why not throw caution to the wind and feel the warm water against your bare skin?

Bents Basin. Aboriginal folklore describes Bents as home to Gurungaty – a large, nasty eel-like creature that drowns and eats outsiders that dare to drink its water. Despite this eerie mythology, Bents is the Wattamolla of the West – a perennially popular place to escape that summer heat.

Bents is a roomy 260m-long, oval-shaped waterhole with murky water on the Nepean River. The Australian Army peculiarly enlarged it in the late 1980s and it's a startling 22m deep.

Norton's Basin & St John's Basin. So immense that it makes you fill your lungs a little more just looking at it, Norton's also provides options for the wild swimmer, as there's another nearby basin and an interconnecting river in which to swim, as well.

As a setting, Norton's Basin is beautiful – nothing bad could be said about – its deep, earthy-brown water, edged by wide rock ledges, or its bush surrounds, where the sounds of a multitude of birds reverberate. Disappointing, however, is the ever-present rubbish. Happily, though, you can always rock-hop 300m upriver to find the much less frequented **St John's Basin** – which definitely profits from being too far from the car park to carry a slab of beer.

When you arrive at St John's, you can't help but gasp at the drama of it all – it's as though the gums have drawn back into the sheer, towering, sandstone cliffs, huddling in on themselves to reveal the basin below.

167 Bents Basin

166 JINGGA POOL

Seclusion: Average-secluded
Navigation: Easy
Descent: 110m
Walk-in: 35 mins, 1.25km, moderate-difficult

ⓘ The thick sandstone slab waterfall that looms over Jingga gives the 65m pool real gravitas. The slab is almost man-made in appearance – its blockish form spans the entire width of the pool. The falls drop almost 5m down the slab's flat face, and the weight of their gushing waters pushes you under as you swim below. There's something about being beneath a waterfall – it only takes a few moments to be made new again!

→ From car park at end of Victoria Rd, Wedderburn, walk through gate into Dharawal National Park and continue along sealed road. After 500m turn R onto steep Jingga Track, which leads directly to the pool.

-34.1636, 150.8377 🔲

167 BENTS BASIN

Facilities: Toilets, picnic tables, wood BBQs, car-based campground
Seclusion: Busy
Walk-in: 2 mins, 100m, easy

ⓘ It's an easy place to get a dose of the bush as you can drive right here, and the air is suffused with the soft echoing crack of bullwhip birds. On summer weekends, though, it gets incredibly busy, and colourful inflatable rings cover the water's surface while boys leap in rapid fire from rock ledges, the most popular of which is 4m. If you're keen on an out-of-hours dip under the starry sky, there's a massive vehicle-based campground with full amenities. Camping fees apply and booking required – contact NPWS.

→ Via car park at end of Bents Basin Rd, Wallacia. Gates open 9am–7pm. Vehicle entry fees apply. Campsite is accessed from Wolstenholme Ave, Greendale. For jump rocks, which can be seen at 2 o'clock when looking directly up the basin, follow path that circuits the water.

-33.9311, 150.6322 🔲🔲🔲🔲

168 NORTON'S & ST JOHN'S BASIN

Seclusion: Busy-secluded
Navigation: Moderate
Descent: 110m
Walk-in: 20 mins, 450m, difficult

ⓘ The Nepean River passes a series of small pools in the boulder-strewn valley connecting the two basins. St John's is almost as big as Norton's, although even more dramatically situated. Here, the river has carved itself a big hole, and the water takes on a shimmering, dancing green from the reflected bush. Swimming here makes you feel very small, and looking up at the trees they seem like spectators looming down from the cheap seats at the MCG.

→ From the end of Nortons Basin Rd, Wallacia, walk through the locked gate and descend the steep, badly eroded fire trail. After 290m turn R onto a path at the second sharp L-hand bend. The path is rough, but leads down to the water's edge. For St John's Basin, boulder-hop upriver on the L bank for 300m.

-33.8582, 150.6174 🔲🔲

And if you have time...

169 SIMMO'S BEACH

Facilities: Toilets, BBQs, playground
Walk-in: 1 min, 50m, easy

ⓘ This pretty little pocket of nature is understandably popular with locals. In the 1950s Simmo's namesake, Bob Simmonds, made a good trade selling illegally mined sand from the Georges River. Thankfully, he left some behind, and this deep bar of white sand hugs a wide, lazy bend of river. It's a good place to bring children, although unfortunately it can experience poor water quality.

➜ Via E end of Fifth Ave, Macquarie Fields. 🚗 1.5km.

-33.9994, 150.9119 🏊 🄲

170 NEPEAN RIVER AT MENANGLE RIVER RESERVE

Walk-in: 2 mins, 100m, easy

ⓘ It's not the Nepean River's fault – this pretty, sandy bend in the river is bordered by reserve and a green patchwork of fields. It could be lovely, but it gets trashy and rowdy here, especially at weekends. Still, it's a decent spot for a swim or cool-off dip if you're passing mid-week.

➜ Via Menangle River Reserve car park off Menangle Rd, Menangle Park (on N side of river).

-34.1186, 150.7406 🏊

171 NEPEAN RIVER AT CAMDEN

Walk-in: 1 min, 50m, easy

ⓘ The banks of the Nepean here are lined with grand oaks and casuarinas – a strange and picturesque mix of Europe and Australia. A charming wooden footbridge spans the 35m river, and the warm, still water is usually deep enough to jump into.

➜ Via E end of Chellaston St, Camden. 🚗 550m.

-34.0611, 150.7013 🏊 🍴

169 Simmo's Beach

171 Nepean River at Camden

Greater Blue Mountains South

Named for the characteristic blue haze that shrouds them, the World Heritage-listed Blue Mountains are as vast as they are beautiful.

Highlights
Great Blue
Mountains South

Our favourites include:

172 Glenbrook Gorge – If you want maximum reward for your effort, you'll do little better than a swim in this spectacular setting.

175 Erskine Creek at Jack Evans – Bring a tent and a friend, for a blissful couple of days of swimming and getting back to nature.

178 Wentworth Falls – Crash, billow, roar. Take an invigorating dip beneath an epic waterfall. The walk here also has some of the best views in the mountains.

183 Kowmung River – It's a long way from Sydney, and it feels like it too, but that's exactly the attraction of this dramatic place.

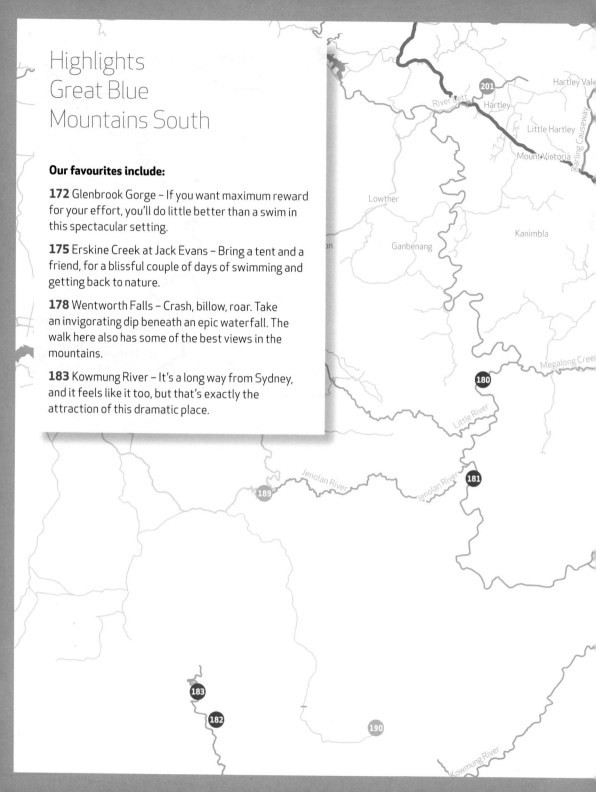

The Great Western Highway wiggles its way west from the Sydney Basin, climbing over 1000m. Either side of the highway, beyond the small towns that cluster along it, is bush and more bush – a million hectares of it! It's one of the largest and most untouched tracts of bushland left in Australia.

To the south, the Blue Mountains National Park meets the untamed Kanangra-Boyd Wilderness. It's in this region that you'll find impressive waterfalls, deep gorges and jaw-dropping vistas. The area is home to the biggest Blue Mountains attractions, yet you'll have no trouble finding a piece of mountains magic for yourself. Many of the swimming delights are within easy reach of Sydney, while others will take you deep into the wild heart of the mountains.

Glenbrook Gorge. In the equation of reward for effort, this is an absolute winner! In every direction the craggy forms of orange and charcoal cliffs rise up towards the sky, hemming you in. You get to swim among this sensational scenery, and yet the walk in is as easy as mountain walks get!

Before reaching the Nepean, Glenbrook Creek first snakes its way between the sandstone ledges and boulders that dominate the gorge. There are channels of interconnecting rapids to play in, dramatically situated, intimate pools, or larger, deep pools for splashing about with friends. Since the gorge runs roughly east-west, the pools get a lot of sun throughout the day.

The gorge is a little too obscure to be visited by the masses of tourists that descend on The Mountains to swim at the nearby, famous Jellybean Pool. Yet at the same time, the walk is not quite challenging enough to entertain the bush-walking set. This means that the gorge is surprisingly little-visited, and the beauty of this place is that once you reach the creek you can walk as little or far as you fancy.

Glenbrook Creek Beach. This large sandbank, on a very sleepy bend of Glenbrook Creek, is the perfect place to spend a lazy weekend. In fact, the only time you'll want to move quickly is to dash from your tent to the water across the hot sand – this place is a real sun trap!

The walk is fairly flat, but involves a bit of rock-hopping and bush-bashing. Happily, there are a number of pools along the way to cool off in, including the large and popular Blue Pool, which marks the start of the walk. Most people actually don't bother to venture this far upstream, making it a quiet spot. ▶

174 Erskine Creek at Big Pool

173 Glenbrook Creek Beach

Glenbrook Gorge

172 GLENBROOK GORGE

Seclusion: Average
Navigation: Moderate
Descent: 120m
Walk-in: 60 mins, 1.7km, moderate

➔ From the Glenbrook NPWS Visitor Centre car park (vehicle entry fees apply), at the S end of Bruce St, Glenbrook, take the road in the bottom-L corner signed Works Depot. After 60m bear R onto Gorge Track. This descends moderately with steps, arriving at a junction close to Glenbrook Creek after 500m. If you turn R here, and then immediately cross the creek over the shrub-covered boulders, on the other side there's a large rock shelf beside a nice, long pool containing some big boulders. Otherwise, continue L downstream, first along a path and then along rock shelf. After 800m there's an easy place to cross where the creek is squeezed between two low boulders in the creek bed – this also happens to be at the start of the gorge – where rocky cliffs come down on both sides. Continue downstream on the shelf. After 1.2km there's a shallow pool nestled among giant boulders. For a while after this pool there's a jumble of boulders and shrubs – it's easier to continue walking near the cliff. After 1.5km the rock shelf ends at a cliff. You may have to cross the creek then re-cross back again. 30m further on there's a long, open pool in spectacular gorge scenery. After 1.7km, there's a large, deepish pool below the cliff on which the train line runs. 🚉 Glenbrook Station 1.3km.

-33.7826, 150.6288 🚶🏊

173 GLENBROOK CREEK BEACH

Facilities: Campsite
Seclusion: Average-secluded
Navigation: Moderate
Descent: 10m
Walk-in: 40 mins, 1km, moderate

➔ From the S end of Bruce Rd, Glenbrook, pass the national park entry station (vehicle entry fees apply), and after 400m park on R. Take the steps from car park. After 130m bear L at the fork. This quickly brings you to Glenbrook Creek. Hop across the rocks to the other side and turn R upstream. A path will soon appear that runs along the side of Blue Pool. After 375m there's another deep pool that has a good rope swing. After 1km you reach a large, open pool on a sharp R-hand bend in the creek. There's a rock platform on this side and the beach is on the other. Optional side trip: if you have a few hours to spare, it's great to explore further upstream. Cross back over the creek from the beach. After a further 1.5km you arrive at a decent pool at the confluence of Glenbrook Creek and Kanuka Brook. 🚉 Glenbrook Station 1.8km.

-33.7756, 150.6092 ⛺🏕🏊♨

174 ERSKINE CREEK AT BIG POOL

Facilities: Campsite
Seclusion: Average-secluded
Navigation: Hard, Penrith GR 747535
Descent: 180m
Walk-in: 60 mins, 1.25km, hard

➔ From the S end of Bruce Rd, Glenbrook, pass the NPWS entry station (vehicle entry fees apply) and continue to cross the Glenbrook Creek causeway, where the road becomes The Oaks Fire

Erskine Creek at Jack Evans

Erskine Creek at Big Pool. Having made it down from Pisgah Rock lookout you'll be elated by the very sight of Big Pool, and will undoubtedly move very quickly to tear off your clothes and dash in.

The pool has a picture-perfect aspect, with the stunning cliffs of Pisgah Rock behind reaching almost all the way up to the clouds. The sonar chiming of bell birds and rushing rapids are all that can be heard while swimming in this delightful 80m-long pool.

If, while swimming, you look up at the sheer-sided sandstone cliffs and the prospect of walking back up is too daunting, well, you can just pitch your tent in the adjacent campsite and tackle it tomorrow!

Erskine Creek at Jack Evans Track. This is such an enticing place to escape the city and spend a weekend – a 200m pool bordered by a large sand bank that's perfect for pitching a tent or two. The bush seems to melt right into the pretty pool, and compared to many swims in The Mountains it's a cinch to get to!

Sculptured cliffs loom over the deep water, and little swallows dart above its surface, harassing dragonflies. In the morning you'll be awoken by a joyful assault of birdsong – when all the birds of the valley chime at once.

You can pepper a couple of idyllic days with lazy swims right here, but for the more adventurous it's also possible to amphibiously explore up and downstream.

▶

Erskine Creek at Jack Evans

174 Erskine Creek at Jack Evans

Bedford Creek at Murphys Glen. What this pool lacks in the full-on Blue Mountains scenery of towering bluffs and expansive vistas, it makes up for in beautiful serenity. It's such a delightful setting – blue gums literally meet the bronze-coloured water, and it's only a relatively short walk to get here.

The pool is long and deep with sandy shallows, so it's perfect for wallowing and soaking in the bush ambiance, as well as for longer swims at a relaxed pace. Despite being tightly enveloped by mature bush, the pool is awash with sunshine, and there's a grassy pad that makes a comfortable place to camp out for the day.

Basic and free camping is available at Murphys Glen campground. Nestled in the bush, it's only 600m from the start of the walk. So why not come for the weekend?

Ingar Dam. With gushing water and warbling birds this place has a real peacefulness to it, but the real draw card is its bush campground. Come here if you like the idea of escaping the city with the family for a weekend of back-to-basics camping, surrounded by the sounds and smells of the bush, and punctuating your day with swims.

The dam was created in the 1960s as a reservoir to aid in local fire-fighting efforts. A tall, cascading waterfall trickles into the 70m long dam, which occupies a sunny hollow, edged by reeds and ferns. The water is not overly deep, making it a good spot for children and paddlers. In the sandy shallows, rope swings dangle from the overhanging trees and allow you to zoom over the inviting, luminous green water. The dam is fed by a complex system of hanging swamps, ensuring that even in times of drought it has a supply of clean water.

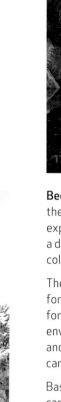

176 Bedford Creek at Murphy's Glen

▶

Bedford Creek at Murphy's Glen

Trail. Keep to this main trail, ignoring turn-offs. After 8km this passes the Oaks Picnic Area and becomes the Nepean Lookout Trail. After 10km park at unsigned lay-by on L, opposite track on R signed Pisgah Rock. The track initially runs fairly level, arriving after 750m at Pisgah Rock, where there are great views of Erskine Creek Gorge. Continue R along the rocks for 20m to an open chimney beside a large banksia. The track descends very steeply down and there are several scrambles. Sometimes the way is unclear, but look out for wear on the rock and scratched arrows. Immediately below the cliffs turn L at a T-junction, just above lush Monkey Ropes Ck. The track winds its way below the cliffs for a short time before gently descending through dense undergrowth directly to the pool, just below the confluence of Erskine and Lincoln Creeks.

-33.8350, 150.5651 🏊🚶🏕

175 ERSKINE CREEK AT JACK EVANS TRACK

Facilities: Campsite
Seclusion: Average-secluded
Navigation: Easy-moderate
Descent: 170m
Walk-in: 50 mins, 1.35km, moderate

➔ From the S end of Bruce Rd, Glenbrook, pass the NPWS entry station (vehicle entry fees apply) and continue to cross the Glenbrook Creek causeway, where the road becomes The Oaks Fire Trail. Keep to this main trail, ignoring turn-offs. After 8km this passes the Oaks Picnic Area and becomes the Nepean Lookout Trail. After 11.8km there's a car park on the R at the end of the trail. Take the track beside the info sign. After 200m there are views over the gorge. Hereafter, the track descends moderately to the creek. At a fork in the track just above the creek bear L downstream. You'll soon see the sand bank on the other side of the creek. After a further 140m, cross over the creek at rapids and walk back upstream to the sandbank. There's also a large campsite

set back in the trees. Note: this pool can get a bit stagnant during drought. However, 125m upstream from the fork is a smaller pool bounded by large boulders, which remains fresh and has a small campsite for a tent or two on its far bank.

-33.8475, 150.5766 🏊🚶🏕⊕

176 BEDFORD CREEK AT MURPHYS GLEN

Facilities: Toilets, car-based campground
Seclusion: Average
Navigation: Moderate
Descent: 100m
Walk-in: 30 mins, 1km, moderate

➔ Via end of Bedford Rd, Woodford. Reset odometer and continue straight onto unsealed road. After 700m pass through gate. After 4km ignore turning R signed to Bedford Creek. After 5.1km, just after descending a long, steep hill, arrive at junction. To swim, turn R and arrive after a further 200m at day-use car park, or for camping turn L and arrive after 400m at Murphys Glen Camping Area. From the day-use car park walk

Wentworth Falls

Empress Falls

The small (free!) campground is very popular, especially on summer weekends and holidays, and it's such a relaxing spot that you'll want to bring your tent so you can enjoy the place to its fullest.

Wentworth Falls. If you need to clear out the cobwebs, a swim beneath these awe-inspiring falls will definitely do the trick! As the falls loom from 187m above, you're immersed in cold water amid a near-deafening rumble; the thrill of it all will leave room for nothing else.

The walk down to the bottom of the falls has stupendous views over Jamison Valley, with the cliff-side track providing one of the most spectacular vantage points in all of the Blue Mountains. Part of the track was made over a hundred years ago by the "Irish Brigade" – a dedicated but clearly crazy lot, who cut steps into the sheer sandstone cliffs to enable safe access into the valley. It's difficult to imagine a steeper walk – the last section involves a series of near-vertical caged ladders, but your efforts are rewarded!

The constant boring of the water plummeting from the falls onto the rocky floor below has created a small pool. Despite the water being bracing even in summer, it's an

177 Ingar Dam

through the bollards and continue along the track. This shortly reaches and then descends parallel to a small creek. After 900m, and with Bedford Creek 10m away, bear L. This soon crosses a large rock ledge above the water and, after 1km, a sandy creek bed. A few metres further is a small clearing on the bank at the end of a long pool.

-33.7724, 150.5001 🏊 ⛺

177 INGAR DAM

Facilities: Toilets, picnic tables, wood BBQs, car-based campground
Seclusion: Busy-average
Walk-in: 1 min, 50m, easy

ⓘ NPWS recommends access by 4WD vehicles only.

→ Bear L at the end of Queen Elizabeth Dr, Wentworth Falls, and continue onto Ingar Fire Trail. After 9.7km bear L at Y-junction to Ingar Day Use & Camping Area. After 10.2km there's a very steep hill which can be wet, and may be unsuitable for 2wd vehicles. Arrive 10.4km.

178 -33.7709, 150.4622 TQD WENTWORTH FALLS

Seclusion: Busy-average
Navigation: Easy-moderate
Descent: 280m
Walk-in: 90 mins, 2.3km, hard

→ Via car park at end of Falls Rd, Wentworth Falls. The walk starts from the info sign near Jamison Lookout. Continue L, signed to Walking Tracks. After 270m you arrive at Wentworth Falls Lookout. The walk takes you down into the valley below the falls. Bear R down the steps signed The Falls and National Pass. This descends gently, and after 620m turn R at T-junction. The steps become steeper from here. After 660m arrive at Fletchers Lookout, which has great views. Turn L and then at Y-junction after 690m, continue R to The Falls. Soon after you cross Jamison Ck with stepping-stones, after which the stairs become even steeper. Soon, after 1.2km, you arrive below the first set of falls, then cross back over the creek. The track then winds its way around the edge of the cliff away from the falls. After 1.6km take the

steps sharp L to Wentworth Pass / Valley of the Waters via Slacks Stairs. This descends seven sets of metal ladders, before switching back L to the base of the second set of falls, where the pool is.
🚉 Wentworth Falls Station 2.4km.

-33.7280, 150.3728 🚶 🚶

179 EMPRESS FALLS

Seclusion: Busy
Navigation: Easy
Descent: 120m
Walk-in: 20 mins, 620m, moderate-hard

ⓘ Owing to the height of Empress Falls, the small circular pool is usually in shadow, making the fortifying effect of the cold even more prominent! There are, however, a few large rocks just downstream that catch the sun and are a good place to warm your goosebump-covered limbs.

→ Via NPWS car park at E end of Fletcher St, Wentworth Falls. The well-signed walk starts from the L-hand side of The Conservation Hut. 🅿 200m.

-33.7207, 150.3592 🚩 🚻

178 Wentworth Falls Pool

Glenbrook Gorge

extraordinary setting for a dip! Swimming allows you to get right up close to the falls – the water billows out, illuminated by the sun, before dropping into the pool hard and fast. Sometimes it feels like a wondrous massage, at other times its sharp points drill into your skin and burn; yet the ebullient experience will leave you wide-eyed and buzzing!

Empress Falls. Swimming beneath these falls is not for the faint-hearted; the water is so exhilaratingly cold that having a dip here is like being slapped silly, and especially after rain the noise from the falls is almost overwhelming! It's impossible to luxuriate, but for a wild, refreshing plunge it's hard to beat.

The falls sit alongside one of the busiest walks in the Blue Mountains. Swimmers are rare, but the falls are a hotspot for wetsuited canyoners, who hop on dangling lines down the falls before dropping the last 5m and dunking like tea bags into the deep pool. There's a good jump rock on the near side of the falls, and as you jump wearing nothing but your swimmers and a brave grin, you'll give cause for passers-by to stare!

▶

180 Coxs River at Bowtells Bridge

178 Wentworth Falls Pool

Coxs River at Bowtells Bridge. From the picturesque Megalong Valley, the historic Six Foot Track leads you down to the Coxs River and this quiet pool – described as an Olympic swimming pool in the bush!

The walk traverses both farmland and national park, taking you through an interesting and rugged landscape where cows graze on bristly pasture and feral goats scamper amongst boulders. At the river, smooth pink-and-grey granite slabs surround the dark water, and are sunny places to lie out on, while willowy river oaks provide shady pockets.

Coxs River at Breakfast Creek. This is remote territory and makes for a magical spot to hide away for a weekend of wild swimming! You might see wild pigs snuffling the moist earth, sunning skinks and snakes, bounding wallabies, rustling lyre birds, and even wild cows grazing along the river bank. You would, however, be quite unlikely to see another person.

The walk in is a hard slog, but if you enjoy bushwalking you will be fully rewarded in exploring this isolated stretch of river! Gone are the little pools and squeezes through granite boulders that characterise the Coxs upriver – here it's much more sleepy. An unusual pyramid-shaped rock borders this ▶

Coxs River at Bowtells Bridge

180 COXS RIVER AT BOWTELLS BRIDGE

Facilities: Toilets at camping area
Seclusion: Average
Navigation: Moderate
Descent: 270m
Walk-in: 135 mins, 6.1km, moderate

ⓘ A little way downriver is a large, grassy campsite set beside the water, so you can stay overnight.

➜ From Megalong Rd, Megalong Valley, 500m S of Old Ford Reserve Campground, turn R into Aspinall Rd and park. Continue along Aspinall Rd on foot. After 850m turn R off road over Guyver Bridge. The track now proceeds through farmland and passes over several stiles. After 2.7km you pass through a gate and then another after 3.5km. The track then descends slowly to the Coxs River. Bowtells Bridge is indicated by a sign saying "alternative bridge when river is high". You can see the pool below from here. If you want to continue on to Coxs River Camping Area, cross the bridge and walk 1km downriver.

-33.7385, 150.1851 🔼 🚶

181 COXS RIVER AT BREAKFAST CREEK

Facilities: Campsite
Seclusion: Secluded
Navigation: Hard, Jenolan GR 388555
Descent: 410m
Walk-in: 210 mins, 8km, hard

ⓘ This walk is unsuitable after heavy rain. Stinging nettles are prolific in one section, making long pants advisable.

➜ Via Dunphys Campground at the end of Megalong Valley Rd, Megalong, approximately 23km south of Blackheath. After passing the Old Ford Reserve campground and the Six Foot Track junction, the road becomes unsealed and passes through a couple of gates and Carlons Farm. Cross the bridge and at the T-junction at the top of the hill turn L. The campground is then on the R. To begin the walk, leave the car park and return back down the hill to the T-junction and take the stile on the L. Head down the fire trail, passing over an old fire trail after 700m. After 800m turn R down another old fire trail. This descends to the usually dry Carlons Creek and then follows it L downstream. There are lots of stinging nettles in this area. After 3.2km you reach Breakfast Creek; turn R and follow downstream. The track crosses the wide, pebbly creek innumerable times – you may lose the track, but it will soon become obvious again. After 3.8km you pass through a gate. The track makes a couple of shortcuts to bypass loops or bends in the creek – once after 4.3km when the track crosses over a spur on the right, and again after 4.8km when it crosses over another spur on the left before reaching the grassy camping area of Frying Pan Flat. Make sure to continue downstream after rejoining the creek each time. Finally, you arrive at Coxs River after about 8km. There's a small pool here or turn L downriver 250m to reach the main pool.

-33.8081, 150.1788 🔼 ↗ 🚫 📷

Morong Falls

attractive 30m pool and the water drops off quickly, becoming deep. You can see further downriver to the poetically-named Wild Dog Mountains rising in the distance. There's a large, coarse sand bank shaded by casuarinas right alongside the river, as well as a grass patch with an elevated view – perfect to pitch a tent on. It's a long, hard walk down here, but why not bring a light overnight pack and make yourself at home, so you can soak in the incredible serenity of this place?

Morong Falls. Kanangra-Boyd National Park is so vast and untamed that it completely dwarfs you. Swimming here, in a deep pool, surrounded by it all, you become a tiny dot. The creek pauses to catch a moment's breath in the pool, before continuing to hurl itself through the wild, primal landscape.

The setting is spectacular, with weighty, imposing granite boulders and the roaring white Morong Falls, which tumble relentlessly. Thanks to the pristine nature of this wilderness area, the dark water is so clean you can drink straight from the pool! It's a delightful place to spend the day – so many waterfalls are fern-encrusted and damp, but here the sun will warm you on your pick of boulders.

If you take your time and exercise caution, it's possible to scramble down the craggy rock drop-offs that the creek tumbles over. Without too much effort you can make it down to the top of the final epic drop-off, which offers a stunning, if dizzying, view of Morong Deep. There are smaller pools below several of the upper waterfalls, which offer further swimming opportunities.

Most of the walk here is on a well-maintained fire trail suitable for mountain biking, so if you've got wheels getting here would be easy.

Kowmung River. This wild river courses through the vast and untrammeled bush of Kanangra-Boyd National Park. It's a primeval landscape of colossal boulders wrought from towering cliffs, and it makes an impressive place for a swim. If you love leaping over rocks and jumping in the water, only to hop out again as you explore further along, this is the place for you!

The Kowmung is one of only seven rivers in NSW that's been declared a wild river – a status only given to rivers in near-pristine condition. It's off the beaten track, remote and generally difficult to access, so gets few visitors. This walk represents the easiest way down to the river, and there's terrific swimming to be had.

▶

183 Kowmung River

183 Kowmung River

You have two options: downriver, at the start of dwarfing **Morong Deep**, the river cuts through the massive granite landscape in small, charging rapids, connecting pool after pool. It's difficult to progress on foot, but it makes the perfect starting point for an aquatic expedition.

Alternatively, upriver, known as **Gridiron Bends**, shallow, pebbly tracts of the Kowmung are peppered with swimming holes. Bushy slopes rise beyond, but there are numerous flats, ideal for pitching a tent or two. Further on, imposing limestone cliffs appear, and if you persevere you'll finally reach spectacular Chardon Canyon, where two creeks meet to form the start of the Kowmung. Both creeks have some deep pools set amid fantastic scenery.

182 Kowmung River

182 MORONG FALLS

Seclusion: Secluded
Navigation: Hard, Kanangra + Shooters Hill GR 765361
Descent: 130m
Walk-in: 90 mins, 4.3km, moderate

➜ From Jenolan Caves Rd turn onto unsealed Kanangra Walls Rd, Kanangra-Boyd NP. Continue for 14.9km, then turn R onto Kowmung River Fire Trail. Reset odometer. After 5.4km turn L onto Morong Creek Fire Trail. Then, after 7.9km, park before a creek crossing. Start the walk by crossing the creek and continuing along the fire trail. After 350m turn R onto Morong Falls Fire Trail. After 1.6km continue through a locked gate. The trail gently undulates before ending at a turning circle. Take path R at 2 o'clock. It's faint and rough, but you soon should hear the sound of the falls. Heading just to the L of them will bring you to the pool after 250m. Be careful to note where you've come from.

-33.9798, 149.9932 🪨🏊🚶

183 KOWMUNG RIVER

➜ From Jenolan Caves Rd turn onto unsealed Kanangra Walls Rd, Kanangra-Boyd NP. Continue for 14.9km, then turn R onto Kowmung River Fire Trail. Reset odometer. After 5.4km ignore L turn for Morong Creek Fire Trail and park after 8.7km at a tuning circle on a sharp, downhill, L-hand bend in the trail, where a sign says "4-wheel drive only".

Morong Deep

Facilities: Campsite
Seclusion: Secluded
Navigation: Hard, Shooters Hill GR 754383
Descent: 220m
Walk-in: 40 mins, 1.7km, moderate

➜ Continue down the fire trail on foot. It descends steeply for 1.4km to a ford on Kowmung River. Cross over the river and turn L downriver. There is no path, but you will pass a small grassy campsite after 500m. 100m further on, a rocky spur will block your way. Leave your gear here to explore downstream.

-33.9601, 149.9796 ⛺◈🌊

Gridiron Bends

Facilities: Campsites
Seclusion: Secluded
Navigation: Hard, Shooters Hill GR 746393
Descent: 220m
Walk-in: 105 mins, 3.4km, moderate

➜ Continue down the fire trail on foot. It descends steeply for 1.4km to a ford on Kowmung River. Turn R and walk upriver. After 500m there's a decent pool on a R-hand bend. The flat, pebbly beach would make a nice campsite. Cross over and continue upriver. After 1.1km there's another small pool on a L-hand bend. Sometime after, cross back over to the R-hand side. At the next bend (a R-hander after 2km) limestone cliffs come down from the L and there's another pool, which also has a shady campsite set back in the trees. Optional side trip: it's possible to continue a further 2.3km upriver to the spectacular Chardon Canyon, just beyond the point where Tuglow River and Hollanders River join to become the Kowmung (Shooters Hill topo map required).

-33.9520, 149.9717 ⛺◈🌊🚶

182 Morong Falls

Kowmung River

Kowmung River

And if you have time...

184 JELLYBEAN POOL

Walk-in: 2 mins, 90m, moderate

ⓘ Close to Sydney and the car park, this is The Mountains' most popular swimming spot. It's relatively small, with a large sand beach for paddlers. Unfortunately, it suffers from graffiti. A little way upstream, a huge boulder protrudes 4m above the water of a deeper pool – it's an excellent jump rock that's popular with teenagers, but generally receives fewer visitors.

→ From Bruce Rd, Glenbrook, pass the national park entry station (vehicle entry fees apply). L after 150m (car park is 750m further). Take steps down to the pool on Glenbrook Creek. 150m further upstream / R along the bank is the jump rock. Train to Glenbrook Station 1.9km.

-33.7815, 150.6190 🚌 🔁

185 CRAYFISH POOL

Navigation: Moderate
Descent: 100m

Walk-in: 40 mins, 935m, moderate

ⓘ A small bowl, hollowed beneath a large waterfall and rock overhang. The surrounding rocks of this shadowy pool are carpeted in downy ferns, and there's a sandy beach. The walk involves a few rocky scrambles, but it's still very popular with families.

→ From end of Bruce Rd, Glenbrook, pass the entry station (vehicle entry fees apply) to cross Glenbrook Creek where road becomes The Oaks Fire Trail. After 7.9km turn R, signed Red Hands Cave. After 3.8km on R, there's small layby to park, with track opposite. This descends above and parallel to a gully. The track is not well made and is unclear at times,. Eventually you reach Kanuka Brook. Turn L here, and walk upstream for just over 100m to the pool.

-33.7833, 150.5692 🥾

186 GLENBROOK CREEK AT MARTIN'S LOOKOUT

Facilities: Campsite
Navigation: Moderate
Descent: 200m
Walk-in: 20 mins, 600m, moderate-hard

ⓘ If you'd like to get out in the bush, yet are pressed for time or feel like taking it easy, then head here. There's a couple of pools to choose from – the one downstream is small and deep, and is quiet. Upstream is a longer, more picturesque pool, with campsite – although it does get passing foot traffic.

→ From car park at end of unsealed Farm Rd, Springwood, take path at 12 o'clock. After 100m arrive at a pretty lookout over Glenbrook Creek. Continue L down stone steps through rocks. This path zig-zags steadily down. After 500m turn L (signed Kings Link). It's just 20m to the creek. Turn L / downstream – the pool is just a further 80m. Return back to the junction above the creek and turn upstream (signed Perch Ponds). After 125m arrive at second pool.

-33.7371, 150.5784 ⛺

187 GLENBROOK CREEK AT THE SWIMMING HOLE

Facilities: Campsite
Navigation: Easy-Moderate
Descent: 180m
Walk-in: 45 mins, 1.2km, moderate

188 Old Wentworth Falls Baths

Kananggra Brook Pool

184 Jellybean Pool

ⓘ A quiet, if unspectacular, bush pool at the junction of two creeks. Small campsite makes for an easy overnighter.

→ From end of Yondell Ave, Springwood, take R, signed Wiggins Track, just before the turning circle – do not take the fire trail straight ahead. The track descends to Sassafras Creek; turn L here and follow it downstream to its junction with Glenbrook Creek. 🅟 400m.

-33.7241, 150.5570 🅰

188 OLD WENTWORTH FALLS BATHS
Navigation: Easy
Descent: 30m
Walk-in: 10 mins, 480m, easy-moderate

ⓘ This 15m pool doesn't have dramatic mountain scenery, but it's a pretty, protected suntrap. Although only thigh-deep, it's still a lovely spot to swim!

→ From Junction of Fletcher St and Jamieson St, Wentworth Falls, take driveway signed Residents Parking Only. At the end of the driveway bear R onto path signed to Charles Darwin Walk. At T-junction after 200m, turn L

and follow Jamison Ck upstream. After 480m a footbridge crosses the creek immediately below the pool.

-33.7189, 150.3770

189 JENOLAN RIVER
Navigation: Easy
Descent: 130m
Walk-in: 40 mins, 1.8km, easy-moderate

ⓘ Jenolan Caves are 340 million years old and a tourist hotspot, but few ever swim in this frigid river. It's culturally significant for Aboriginal groups who believed the waters had curative powers, and their sick would travel to bathe in the mineral-dense water. There's a pool with a tumbling waterfall, while downstream a dam has created a large pool with astonishingly clear water. It's a quiet, pleasant spot, with wispy trees and pockets of grass.

→ From Jenolan Caves car park, Jenolan Caves Rd, walk down past hotel, through the Grand Arch to the Blue Lake. Take path to R of lake – where swimming is not permitted. Ignore the path L after the lake. Shortly you'll arrive at waterfall and

first pool after 850m. The water is too shallow to jump safely from the waterfall. The dam is a further 950m downriver.

-33.8199, 150.0275 🅽

190 KANANGRA BROOK POOL
Navigation: Easy-moderate
Descent: 50m
Walk-in: 25 mins, 800m, moderate

ⓘ A tiny, 2m plunge pool, a stone's throw from a heart-stopping drop-off into Kanangra Gorge. The water is so bracing that a quick dip will more than suffice!

→ Follow unsealed Kanangra Rd, Kanangra-Boyd National Park, for duration (27km from junction with Jenolan Caves Rd). Take track ahead through locked gate for 500m to end, pausing en route to admire the view of Kanangra Walls. A track L descends via well-made steps to Kalang Falls, which has a pool beneath it, although it often has a lot of bush debris and is a bit too public to have a relaxing swim. If you rock-hop downstream for a further 50m you arrive at Kanangra Brook Pool.

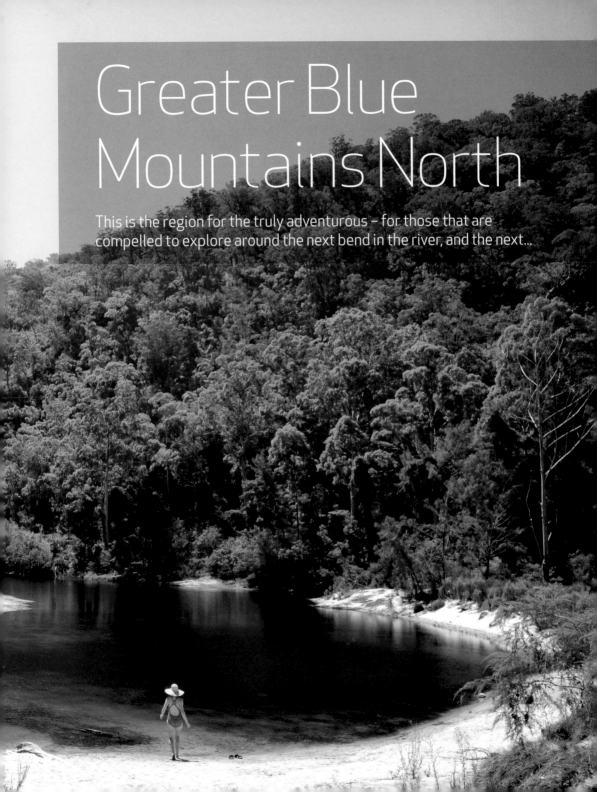

Greater Blue Mountains North

This is the region for the truly adventurous – for those that are compelled to explore around the next bend in the river, and the next...

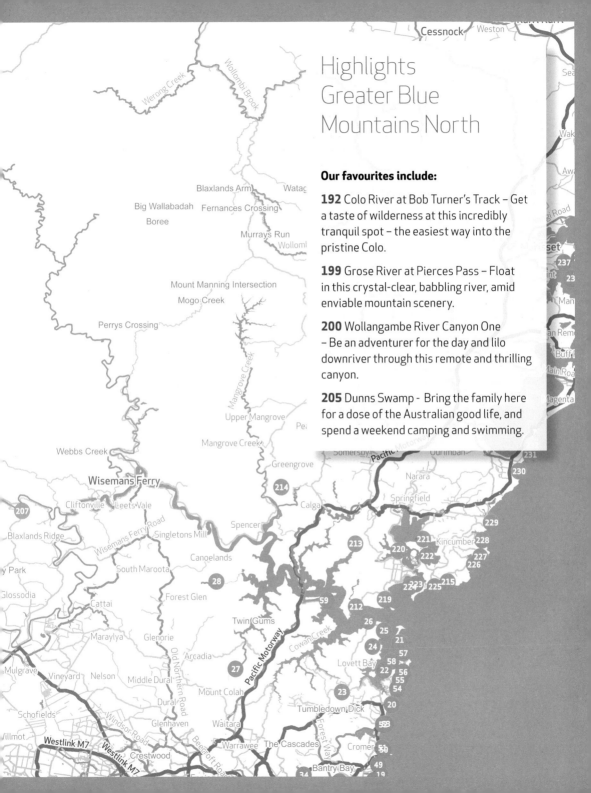

Highlights
Greater Blue
Mountains North

Our favourites include:

192 Colo River at Bob Turner's Track – Get a taste of wilderness at this incredibly tranquil spot – the easiest way into the pristine Colo.

199 Grose River at Pierces Pass – Float in this crystal-clear, babbling river, amid enviable mountain scenery.

200 Wollangambe River Canyon One – Be an adventurer for the day and lilo downriver through this remote and thrilling canyon.

205 Dunns Swamp - Bring the family here for a dose of the Australian good life, and spend a weekend camping and swimming.

Colo River at Tootie Creek

193 Colo River at Tootie Creek

To the north of the Great Western Highway, the Blue Mountains National Park meets the boundless Wollemi Wilderness.

NSW has only five wild rivers – a title reserved for the most pristine and untouched – and two of them course through the bush here, passing through eye-popping canyons and rugged valleys. While the region offers some easy bush experiences, many locations are isolated and remote, and the rewards for the intrepid swimmer are great!

Colo River at Canoe Creek. This is somewhere you'll never forget. Neither is it a place you can just happen upon, and this remoteness adds to its special feeling. Here, the Colo manoeuvres around a dogleg bend beneath grand sandstone cliffs, and it makes for a breathtaking setting for a swim. It's a truly memorable spot!

Such is the beauty of the Colo that it breeds a particular type of fanatic. Many make annual pilgrimages here, and are ever keen to turn others on to this pristine wilderness. The craggy cliffs are so tall you need to arch your head all the way back to catch a glimpse of the sky. The golden river can be shallow during times of low rainfall, although there remain pockets deep enough for short swims. It's such a great spot that you should allow time to explore up and downriver, so make use of one of the large sandbanks and camp.

Colo River at Bob Turner's Track. The scenery here may not be as dramatic as at nearby Canoe Creek, but Bob Turner's Track is by far the easiest way down into the rugged Colo Wilderness. What's more, the river here is always deep and excellent for swimming, even in times of drought.

This sleepy bend in the Colo is bounded by wide sandbanks, bleached white by the sun, with pockets of shady casuarinas. While you can easily spend a day happily swimming right here, there's also the option of exploring smaller pools up and downriver. The sandbanks are an ideal place to pitch your tent, and there's plenty of room for multiple camping parties.

Colo River at Tootie Creek. The wilderness has a particular luring call that's inextricably linked with solitude. You will most likely have this piece of wilderness to yourself.

▶

191 Colo River at Canoe Creek

191 COLO RIVER AT CANOE CREEK
Facilities: Campsite
Seclusion: Average-secluded
Navigation: Hard, Colo Heights GR 743140
Descent: 400m
Walk-in: 135 mins, 3.5km, hard
ⓘ The walk down is not especially long, but it's one of the hardest in the book, involving a couple of tricky rock scrambles. Most people stay at least overnight, and it's difficult to imagine having a morning swim in a more dramatic and idyllic spot!

→ From the service station on Putty Rd, Colo Heights, continue N for approximately 16km, then turn sharp L onto fire trail, marked with a Wollemi National Park sign. Continue for 8km to car park at locked gate. Proceed past gate along Grassy Hill Fire Trail for approximately 2km. About 10m before a turning circle, take unmarked track on L. It initially descends gently, but becomes progressively steeper. There are some difficult scrambles as the path drops into the gully of Canoe Ck, before arriving at a large sandbank beside the river.
-33.2900, 150.5751 🔺

192 COLO RIVER AT BOB TURNER'S TRACK
Facilities: Campsite
Seclusion: Average-secluded
Navigation: Easy
Descent: 260m
Walk-in: 90 mins, 3.5km, moderate
→ From the service station at Colo Heights, continue N for 700m, then turn L, signed Bob Turners Fire Trail. Continue for another 2.7km to car park (not at the trail head). Take the steps signed Bob Turners Walking Track. This well-made track descends moderately, crossing several small gullies, and leads directly to the river.
-33.3739, 150.6657 🏊 🔺

193 COLO RIVER AT TOOTIE CREEK
Facilities: Campsite
Seclusion: Secluded
Navigation: Hard, Mountain Lagoon GR 825028
Descent: 440m
Walk-in: 120 mins, 2.55km, hard
→ From Mountain Lagoon Rd, Mountain Lagoon, turn L onto Sams Way. After 1.3km turn L onto fire trail (signed Walking Tracks, Tootie Creek, Colo Meroo) and follow the signs for Tootie Ck for a little over 5km to end. The track from the car park descends gently along a spur – it's often indistinct, but there are no turn-offs and there are occasional star picket markers. After 1.8km you arrive at a spectacular lookout on the edge of the Colo Gorge. Your destination is the rapids far below. The track from here switchbacks L past an impressive bridging boulder. There's a lot of flood debris just before you reach the sandbank and river, which you must pick through. It's a good idea to leave an exit marker for yourself before you go off to explore. On your return trip, note that at the rock outcrop above the lookout, keep along the spur line, ignoring a fake trail L.
-33.3919, 150.6622 🏊 🔺 🚶

Colo River at Bob Turner's Track

The track that leads down to the river is not particularly well known, and the walk is a hard slog, helping make this the least visited of the Colo River swims featured in this book. Set below rapids, it's a fantastically quiet spot, with sandy shallows and a 100m-long, deep pool. On the opposite bank, craggy cliffs almost conquer the sky, while a large sandbank edges the pool and makes a terrific spot to camp overnight

Grose River at Waterboard Fire Trail. The scenery here is ridiculously pretty – enormous, mast-like blue gums line the river, and their ghostly grey trunks form a striking contrast with the vivid bush beyond. Despite being the Grose's most easily accessible point, this tranquil spot is little visited and makes a superb place to spend the day.

The Grose here is exceedingly languid. It seems to have decided that after all that rushing down through the mountains, it will savour the wonderful valley scenery for just a while longer before having to sully itself with the murky ▶

195 Grose River at Faulconbridge Point

195 Grose River at Faulconbridge Point

196 Paradise Pool

Hawkesbury just a few kilometres downstream. The mere gentlest of breezes appear to make it change direction and head back up towards the mountains.

The walk follows a fire trail that was established to enable testing of the Lower Grose Valley for its suitability to dam. Thankfully, the dam never went ahead and the Grose remains intact. The rich gold water is rather shallow, although there are some deeper navigable channels for swimming. It's such a beautiful spot, though, that it's actually quite wonderful just kicking back in the shallows and soaking in the ambiance!

Grose River at Faulconbridge Point. Often, even when you think you're a long way from civilisation, you can still hear the occasional squeal of semi-trailer air brakes, or the roar of a motorbike; but here, nope. It's just cicadas, bell birds and the gush of the Grose.

If you're feeling fit, and want to get away from it all, this is a great place to head. Situated deep within the little-visited Lower Grose Valley, getting here involves one of the longest walks in the book. However, with a bicycle you could easily knock off the first 5.5km. This section of the walk is very exposed, with minimal shade, so aim to spend the hottest part of the day at the pool.

The track leads you directly to a large pool on a bend in the Grose. The pool's shimmering surface is dark and opaque next to the brilliant green of the encroaching bush. Spend a day wading in and out of the water, diving off rocks and floating on your back breathing in the summer. It's a wonderfully scenic spot and a real sight for sore eyes.

Paradise Pool. There are many place names around Sydney that seem an exaggeration or are perhaps a reflection of former glory – but Paradise Pool is not one of them. It really lives up to its name!

In half an hour you're transported to what feels like the middle of the bush; just 1km from the suburban streets of Linden, this pool is an unexpected delight that, incredibly, few seem to know about.

A classic 15m-diameter waterhole in a hollow, with sandy beach and sun-drenched rock platforms, it makes a lovely

▶

194 Grose River at Waterboard Fire Trail

194 GROSE RIVER AT WATERBOARD FIRE TRAIL

Seclusion: Secluded
Navigation: Moderate-hard, Kurrajong GR 813775
Descent: 150m
Walk-in: 50 mins, 2km, moderate

→ From the end of Cabbage Tree Rd, Grose Wold, continue onto the fire trail and take the second L after 750m, which after 50m arrives at a car park. Walk through gate onto the Water Board Fire Trail. Follow this gently down, then gently up, ignoring numerous turn-offs, until you reach a major fork with a single tree in the middle. Take L fork. This soon starts to descend steeply for 1km. It's very rough, but flattens out parallel to the river. 50m after a concrete paved section, look out for a steep path descending to the L. This quickly brings you to a wide sandy bank after 50m. Make sure to take your bearing if you leave this spot.

-33.6201, 150.6434

195 GROSE RIVER AT FAULCONBRIDGE POINT

Seclusion: Average-secluded
Navigation: Moderate
Descent: 400m
Walk-in: 165 mins, 6.75km, moderate

→ Travel along Grose Rd, Faulconbridge for 3.5km from junction with Great Western Hwy to car park before locked gate. Continue on foot past the gate for approximately 5.5km. Just before a turning island on the L side of the fire trail, a track branches off to the R – it's faintly marked "Grose" in white on a rock (if you're feeling enthusiastic you can continue a further 1km to the impressive lookout). Take this track and continue until you reach the pool – approximately 1.25km. This part of the track descends steeply and is rocky in parts with some scrambling required. Thankfully, the track levels to a more gradual descent for a few hundred metres before the final 150m scramble. 🚉 Faulconbridge Station 4.8km.

-33.6230, 150.5810 🏊 🧗

196 PARADISE POOL

Seclusion: Average
Navigation: Moderate
Descent: 100m
Walk-in: 35 mins, 1.1km, moderate

→ Heading W, turn off Great Western Hwy at Tollgate Dr, Linden. Cross over bridge and park on roadside, just past junction with Glossop Rd. Walk back to Tollgate Dr. Turn L on Glossop Rd after 50m, then next L onto Caley Ln after 140m. Turn R into an empty block signed Caley's Repulse after 180m. Head up through the block between houses, and at the ridgetop, after 240m, turn R along a fire trail. After 410m turn L onto a path signed Blue Mountains NP, keeping straight over the rock outcrop. After 580m bear L at T-junction and continue steeply downhill. The path crosses a small creek after 860m and soon after reaches another T-junction – turn R. This runs level, downstream, parallel to the creek before arriving above the pool. 🚉 Linden Station 1.2km.

-33.7136, 150.4882 🍴 🚉

Edenderry Falls

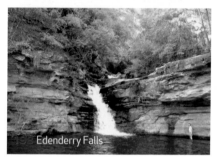
Edenderry Falls

spot to spend the day. From the beach, the water drops off suddenly and it's particularly deep below the pretty waterfall, which provides a 5m jump.

Grand Canyon. The walk through the Grand Canyon is one of the most popular in all of the Blue Mountains. However, most visitors stick to the official track and completely miss out on experiencing the most magnificent section of the canyon. You'll be forgiven for feeling a touch of smugness when, just nearby, walkers are taking in the mountain air elbow-to-elbow – while here, in this gorgeous cathedral of stone and water, it's just you. The 30m pool is as long as the canyon walls are high. As you look up at the slit of sky, high, high above, it's easy to feel a sense of awe.

As you'd imagine, the pool gets little sunshine and the water is gaspingly cold. This ensures that a quick lap will more than satisfy. Of course, the scenery compensates for any discomfort, and anyway, when you immerse yourself in cold water you quickly become dosed up on a cocktail of feel-good chemicals!

Edenderry Falls. Often the promise of a summer swim in the Blue Mountains means a serious walk in, before steeling yourself for a hot walk out. For much of this walk, however, you're accompanied by the reassuring gurgling of Greaves and Govetts Creeks. And, while it's a long walk to the deep and mysterious Edenderry Falls, this out-of-the-way spot makes a perfect end destination and certainly warrants the effort!

The initially busy track passes several pools like a line of dominoes: small waterfalls tumble into pools, before meeting rocky drop-offs and tumbling again into pools further downstream. Some are shallow and sun-drenched, while others are deeper with sunlight only filtering through the thick bush canopy. Here, you leave the tourist set and take the path less travelled to discover the little-visited Edenderry Falls.

A 30m pool sits in a bowl beneath the falls, and dramatic, towering cliffs loom beyond. The water is unfathomable and always tits-freezing! There are a few rocks to sit on, but as it's rarely in sunshine, it's not a place to spend the day – and once you've made your way here and had a swim it will probably be time to head for home. ▶

197 Grand Canyon

197 GRAND CANYON

Seclusion: Average
Navigation: Moderate
Descent: 200m
Walk-in: 60 mins, 1.75km, moderate

ⓘ The walk also takes in a couple of other pools, which make for nice appetisers en route – but don't get so cold that you miss out on the main show!

→ From the end of Evans Lookout Rd, Blackheath, take R track, signed Grand Canyon. This descends a cliff-lined gully on a well-made track with steps. After 1km the track levels as you reach Greaves Creek. Turn R, and you're at the lower end of the Grand Canyon. After a couple of minutes you arrive at a remarkable pool, half covered by a massive boulder into which tumbles a small waterfall. Continue for another 10 mins and there's a long pool on the L of the track. A couple of minutes further, the track exits L up out of the canyon – ignore this and continue along the canyon. Rock-hop to cross the creek. There's a lot of log debris. On the R-hand side you see an old flight of stairs carved

into the rock. Ascend these and then drop back down to the creek. Walk up the creek and soon you arrive at a 20m-long, deep pool in a narrow section – it's about 10 mins from where you left the main track.

-33.6597, 150.3202 🚶

198 EDENDERRY FALLS

Seclusion: Secluded
Navigation: Hard, Katoomba GR 537738
Descent: 600m
Walk-in: 165 mins, 3.75km, hard

ⓘ This walk can be combined with visiting the Grand Canyon.

→ From car park at end of Evans Lookout Rd, Blackheath, take R track signed Grose Valley Walks. After 70m you reach Evans Lookout with fantastic; and perhaps daunting, views – Edenderry Falls is located in the second side-valley on the R. From here you descend on a fancy new track through a cliff-lined gully. After 1km the track levels as you reach Greaves Creek at the bottom end of the Grand Canyon. Cross over the creek and turn L downstream, following signs to the Grose Valley. From here the track

is not as well made and is sometimes faint. Soon the track crosses back over the creek, then descends below a cliff and zigzags over a landslide. You may wish to turn R here to look at noisy Beauchamps Falls, before continuing down the landslide through a tunnel between large boulders. A little further, carved stone steps pass through two big boulders and 5m after is a decent small pool. After 2.1km the track crosses back to the R side of the creek again where there are bent metal rods in the creek bed. A little further there's a pretty pool under a small waterfall. From here the descent becomes more gradual. After 2.85km cross back over the creek to the L side. 50m after the crossing, look out for an overgrown path turning R. Follow this for 150m to its end at the junction of Greaves Creek and Govetts Creek, where there's a small pool. Cross over Greaves Creek and pick up a faint path that runs diagonal to both creeks for about 70m to a point about 50m from both creeks where there's a small, unpermitted campsite. The path from here is easier to follow: it proceeds quite flatly, parallel up

199 Grose River at Pierces Pass

200 Wollangambe River Canyon One

Grose River at Pierces Pass. The Grose River descends down the valley to the lower reaches of the mountains, and by the time it's made its way to Faulconbridge Point, it's sedate and meandering. Here, though, it feels as it is – a mountain river – gurgling, active, and bloody crisp! Swimming here, you're right in the middle of classic Blue Mountains scenery, and as you gaze up there can be no doubt of where in the world you are!

Pierces Pass is well graded and one of the easiest ways to access the Grose Valley. The route has a long history of use, both by local Aboriginals and later as a stock route to the Blue Gum Forest. With wonderful views of the sheer walls of Mount Banks and Mount Hay, it's also one of the most scenic walks in The Mountains, and while it gets a few visitors, it's definitely not on the tourist map.

The valley walls are only 1.5km apart, which is actually close enough to really feel their presence – especially considering the almost 500m descent. The river bustles around large boulders, pausing temporarily in sunlit pools, where the pale green water is so fantastically clear that you appear to be levitating as you float.

Wollangambe River Canyon One. This is for those that want to shake off the monotony of city life and be an adventurer for a day. This section of canyon on the Wollangambe River is popular, but such is its beauty and otherworldliness that it's easy to still feel like you're the first person to ever venture here. With water of changing hues and looming, sculptured canyon walls, the scenery is knockout. Travelling this canyon makes for a challenging day, but the pioneering spirit it arouses can't be beat!

The pristine waters of the Wollangambe flow through this narrow canyon in the untamed Wollemi Wilderness. The water is chilly, and even in summer you need to wear a wetsuit. The only way to experience this otherwise inaccessible environment is by lilo – simply recline and gently paddle with your hands downriver. It's a lot of fun and also limits your exposure to the cold. Anytime you want to experience the river by being in it and swimming, just park up your lilo and hop in! Water dragons are very common on the rocks and they often jump in and join you.

You travel through changing sections of the canyon – some illuminated with dancing rays of sunshine, where steam ▶

200 Wollangambe River Canyon One

Govetts Creek 10-30m away. Edenderry Falls and pool are another 600m. It's necessary to boulder hop upstream the final 50m. It can't be accessed from above as it sits in an amphitheatre.

-33.6471, 150.3450 🚩📷🚶

199 GROSE RIVER AT PIERCES PASS

Seclusion: Average-secluded
Navigation: Moderate
Descent: 480m
Walk-in: 90 mins, 2.3km, moderate

ⓘ This walk takes in two pools: hidden by screens of bush, they're perfect places for swimming in the buff.

→ Via Bells Line of Road – on the R 9.9km E from Bell, or on the L 10.1km W from Mt Tomah. Unsealed road is signed Pierces Pass Picnic Area. Drive 1km to car park at end, ignoring L turn to the lookout. Take the track signed Pierces Pass. The descent is consistently downhill on a well-graded track with some steps. Ignore path that leads down R to a creek after 640m. There are terrific views of the cliffs both sides of the valley. After 2.3km the track arrives at the river. Cross

over to the track that runs parallel to the river. There is a pool 90m downstream – you'll notice a large sloping boulder 5m from the track. There's a deeper, more secluded pool 65m upstream from the crossing – walk up the track and cut across to the river from a little (unpermitted) fire circle beside the track on the R.

-33.5804, 150.3368 🚶

200 WOLLANGAMBE RIVER CANYON ONE

Seclusion: Average
Navigation: Hard, Mt Wilson + Wollangambe GR 546914
Descent: 300m
Walk-in: 90 mins, 2.6km, hard
Walk-out: 105 mins, 2.9km, hard
Lilo: 4–5 hours, 2.3km

→ From Mt Wilson Fire Station car park, The Avenue, Mt Wilson, take fire trail near info sign that leads behind the station. After 200m turn L at a T-junction. The trail ascends, before descending to another T-junction after 700m. Turn R here, and then after just 50m, turn L onto a path.

You pass this junction on your return journey. The path descends gently to a large rock pagoda with views after 1.9km. Do not turn L here, instead stay R keeping the next outcrop on your L-hand side. After 2.2km the path turns sharp L. This contours for 150m before descending into a deep gully, which leads to the river. There are a couple of flat rocks on which to blow up your lilo and get into your wetsuit. Near the start there's an open and sunny section of canyon with cliffs for jumping – check water depth. Don't hurry past this bit. Soon after, there's a long block-up that takes half an hour to get through. Here you'll find some sandy beaches that make good places to stop for lunch. In the last part of the canyon there are a few smaller block-ups to get through. The exit (-33.4869, 150.3746) is fairly obvious – at the end of a long, narrow, straight stretch you'll see a sheer cliff perpendicular to the canyon – at a distance it appears to block the way. There are tree-filled gaps in the cliffs on both sides, and a tiny yellow arrow sign R points the way out, R. The climb out of the canyon begins with a couple of steep,

billows off your wetsuit; others dark and mysterious, where you can almost touch the walls on both sides. The water is sometimes very deep, and there are some amazing rock ledges to jump from.

At times you need to carry your lilo as you scramble over rocks and wade in shallow water before the river opens up again, but most of the time you can just lay back and enjoy the brilliant scenery. The Wollangambe continues on through the canyon beyond this exit, but if you still want more you can always tackle the next section (Wollangambe Two) tomorrow!

Access to the river is from the charming village of Mount Wilson, and as an early start is essential, your best bet is to come for a weekend and stay in the free campground or one of its B&Bs. Allow plenty of time to complete the journey (leave the fire station before 9am). Do not head off if rain is forecast, or if there's been recent heavy rain, as the river level can rise extremely quickly. Travel in a small group. Let someone know your intentions, and consider taking a Personal Locator Beacon. The water is cold, even in summer. A wetsuit and shoes with good grip are essential. Put warm clothes, food and instructions in dry packs, inside a large backpack – this will serve as a back rest on your lilo. The best lilos are the blue, inflatable, single mattresses available from the likes of Kmart and Target. Take a spare, as well a puncture repair kit among your group.

River Lett at Hyde Park Reserve. Just on the other side of the mountains is the gurgling River Lett. This area is significant to Aboriginal groups, who consider it a sacred women's place. For the swimmer it's a lovely spot, little known other than by locals, and it's just a five minute walk from the car park.

Most of Sydney is sandstone, such that swimmers are never far away from it, so the pink-and-grey granite here comes as quite a shock! The velvety brown water squeezes itself around boulders and over ramps, connecting the main pool with smaller ones up and downstream.

Although it's enclosed by bush, the river is very open and sun-drenched. Despite being popular, there are masses of warm slabs to lie on, as well as plenty of nooks and crannies to hide away if you want.

Clarence Dam. This is a veritable wild swimming fun park – there are countless rope swings and ledges from which to fling yourself into the deep water. And if the thought of an ▶

Nayook Canyon at Deep Pass

Nayook Canyon at Deep Pass

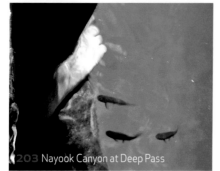
203 Nayook Canyon at Deep Pass

11m jump makes your stomach do back-flips, Clarence Dam is still a stunning place for a swim. Also, unlike most other Blue Mountains swimming holes, you can pretty much drive right here – so what's not to love?

The dam is a deep, flooded canyon, historically used to provide water for the steam trains at nearby Zig-Zag Railway. These days, it's famed for a high and straight, 40m-long natural cliff that has perfect, stair-like access to its top, making it seem like it was purpose-built for jumping. Although signs in the reserve stress the dangers, unsurprisingly, it's still incredibly popular.

While not wanting to understate the thrill of a good jump, what's equally remarkable is just how beautiful it is here. The water gently winds its way around the curves of the old canyon, its near-black water mirroring the sky and bush for a meandering 300m! If you're partial to long swims, but aren't keen on laps, this could be your place.

Nayook Canyon at Deep Pass is a magical place of light and shadow, of jumping into deep pools and exploring around the next corner, and it's highly recommended!

▶

201 River Lett

tricky scrambles. After this the going gets easier, but it's a continuous ascent for about an hour / 1.4km before reaching a fire trail. Turn right here and ascend a bit more. After 2.2km you pass the path junction where you descended to the canyon. Turn L 50m further on and then R to get back to the car park.

-33.4888, 150.3592 🟥🗑️🚶

201 RIVER LETT, HYDE PARK RESERVE

Seclusion: Busy-average
Navigation: Easy
Descent: 30m
Walk-in: 5 mins, 350m, easy
ⓘ Access road may be impassable after rain.

➜ Turn R off the Great Western Hwy onto Mid Hartley Rd, Hartley, 8.4km from the centre of Mt Victoria. After 350m turn L onto unsigned and unsealed Hyde Park Lane, and follow for 1.9km to car park. A path leads down to the river from the far end.

-33.5318, 150.1871 🟦

202 CLARENCE DAM

Seclusion: Busy-average
Navigation: Easy
Descent: 40m
Walk-in: 5 mins, 200m, moderate
ⓘ As with all jumping hotspots, Clarence Dam is a bogan magnet, so it can get pretty ugly – arrive early or come during the week outside of school holidays. Fair warning! Access road may be impassable after rain.

➜ From Bell, drive W on Chifley Rd for 6.3km, then turn L onto unsealed road just before the road crosses over train tracks (if you reach the R turn to Clarence Colliery you've gone 500m too far). Turn immediately R and drive parallel to the train tracks for 400m before reaching a locked gate. Reset your trip meter and turn L. At the T-junction after 100m turn R. After 800m, at a three-way split, bear R. After 1.2km, at a turning circle (this may be the future car park), turn L and continue, ignoring side roads. After 1.4km arrive at car park. Take descending track on R.

-33.4830, 150.2501 🟦🟥

203 NAYOOK CANYON AT DEEP PASS

Facilities: Toilet, Deep Pass camping
Seclusion: Busy-average
Navigation: Moderate
Descent: 100m
Walk-in: 60 mins, 1.55km, hard
ⓘ Access road may be impassable after rain.

➜ From Bell, drive W on Chifley Rd for 7.9km onto unsealed road signed Zig Zag Railway. Reset odometer. After 100m turn R at T-junction signed Newnes State Forest Road. At T-junction after 8.7km turn R on Glowworm Tunnel Rd. After 20.4km turn R, slightly uphill, onto a wide road. After 21.4km turn L at the T-junction. The road gets rougher from here. Keep to the main route, ignoring turn-offs. After 22.9km bear L at fork. After 24km turn R at fork. After 26.5km you should arrive at the car park. (Note this is the southern car park. There is also a northern car park, but it's only accessible by 4WD). Take the track beside the info sign. It descends a very rough fire trail for 300m before flattening and bearing L on a narrow overgrown path

204 Capertee River

202 Clarence Dam

Dunns Swamp

Nayook Creek courses through the narrow canyon before reaching the open grassy flat of Deep Pass Campground. The journey here to the edge of the Wollemi Wilderness – first by car through the maze of increasingly rough forestry roads and then on foot – only adds to the sense of adventure. Anchored ropes help get you up and down the trickier scrambles of the canyon, and you'll need to shimmy along a couple of floating log bridges. Although a degree of fitness and agility is required, Nayook is an easy introduction to canyons.

The canyon contains a number of deep pools. As with most canyons, the water is perishingly cold, and unless you're a masochist, a quick dunk will be enough of a swim to leave you feeling fantastic! The best pool has a high, plunging waterfall, which mists the fern-dotted cliff face, creating intense rainbows. There are several rock ledges that provide excellent jumping opportunities – although the water is not deep enough to jump into from the top of the waterfall.

Although it's an effort to get here, it's well worth it – so why not cart along some friends and a tent and stay for the weekend? The campsite is one of the prettiest in Sydney – a protected bowl of downy grass with a creek and fire-circle. All this has not gone unnoticed, so don't expect to have it to yourself! ∎

205 Dunns Swamp

which descends more gently between cliffs, and then through a wider valley for another 700m before reaching the campsite of Deep Pass. 1km total. To get to the canyon keep the main fire pit and some cliffs on your R – turn L up a grassy path, pass the small ruins of the old farmhouse on your L, then descend and follow the path across Nayook Creek. Soon after turn L, walking upstream parallel to the creek (which is unseen). 350m from the campsite you reach the start of the canyon with cliffs on both sides. It's another 100m to the first pool and a further 100m to the main pool. From here the canyon continues for another 500m. Return to Chifley Rd directions: After 2.5km ignore R turn. At 3.6km bear R. At 4.4km bear L. At 5.2km you reach the start of the pine forest; turn R. At T-junction after 6.1km turn L. At 17.7km turn L.

-33.3431, 150.3059 🅼🅰🖳🏃

204 CAPERTEE RIVER, COORONGOOBA

Facilities: Toilet, wood BBQs, car-based campground

Seclusion: Secluded
Navigation: Moderate
Descent: 0m
Walk-in: 75 mins, 1.9km, moderate
→ Turn L off Glen Alice Rd, Glen Davis, onto Goora Rd (not on Google Maps) just after the town sign. After 250m turn R onto unsealed Nioka Street. After 3km there's a ford crossing, which may be impassable after rain. The campground is about 5km from Glen Alice Rd. The walk starts from the far end of the campground – follow the vehicle track until it runs out after a short distance. Cross the river here and continue downriver. There's no path, but it's fairly easy going with some rock scrambling and a little bush bashing. After 500m there is a not particularly attractive 400m-long, deep pool which ends in a rapid. After this there's a series of about half a dozen smaller, nicer pools often bounded by boulders. These pools continue to the junction with Freshwater Creek, which comes in on the R.

-33.1390, 150.3342 🏃🅻🚫🅰

205 DUNNS SWAMP

Facilities: Toilets, picnic tables, wood BBQs (fees), car-based campground
Seclusion: Busy-average
Navigation: Moderate
Ascent: 10m
Walk-in: 20 mins, 900m, easy

ⓘ If you're up for a bit of a scramble, the impressive, far-reaching views from the pagoda lookout are worth the effort. Camping fees apply – contact NPWS.

→ From unsealed Narango Rd, Olinda, follow signs to Wollemi National Park. From the main car park turn L along the track signed Weir Walk. After 370m you reach Platypus Point, where low rock juts out into the water. This is a good place to swim. Continuing on, after 100m the track bends sharp R, then descends into a little dip. Shortly after ascending again, take the small path R. This leads after 300m to the R-hand side of a narrow-necked peninsula where there's a cliff that leans out over the water 900m. The other side of the peninsula is just 75m away, and is very pretty and also a quieter spot for a swim.

-32.8349, 150.2014 🏊🅼🅰

205 Dunns Swamp

Capertee River at Coorongooba. It's amazing that the Capertee Valley is not more well known. As one of the world's longest canyons, second only to the Grand Canyon in Arizona, the scenery is pretty awe-inspiring!

The drive from Glen Davis to Coorongooba Campground takes you through farmland, where plains of long yellow grass, dotted with grazing cows, join seamlessly with flat-topped cliffs that rise up to meet the enormous sky – it's without doubt one of the most dramatic around Sydney!

The free campground is one of the most beautiful in the region. It's a large car-based site on the grounds of a former farm, and the grassy flats shadowed by the lofty canyon walls are full of kangaroos at dusk. The Capertee River edges the campground, but here it's too shallow for swimming. Further downstream, however, the river deepens, and is characterised by boulder-bounded pools, interspersed with rapids and glimpses of the spectacular cliffs. It's a great platypus habitat, so keep your eyes open. Perhaps because there's no formal track, it's also little visited.

Dunns Swamp. This 3km serpentine length of water is bordered by cliffs, rock pagodas and pockets of reeds in which moorhens hoot and dragonflies flicker. Known as "Ganguddy" to the local Wiradjuri people, the name Dunns Swamp is a bit misleading as it's actually a dammed section of the Cudgegong River, with deep, dark brown water that feels silky on the skin. Dunns was created in the 1920s to provide water for Kandos cement works, yet despite its industrial beginnings the landscape is striking – and it's a smashing place for a swim!

One thing you notice about Dunns is that it's startlingly quiet – with water so still there's not even the usual faint babble, just a sprinkling of chirruping birds filters through the thick silence. The absolute stillness of the water also make it excellent for settling into a meditative rhythm and swimming leisurely along its length, or dropping a lilo in for a lazy paddle.

The river adjoins a large busy campground, but you shouldn't have trouble finding a place to yourself if you're seeking solitude. Although jumping and diving are prohibited throughout the entire Wollemi National Park, it hasn't gone unnoticed that the rock ledges jutting out over very deep water are seemingly made for it – one spot facing Platypus Point is particularly popular.

And if you have time...

206 COLO RIVER, UPPER COLO RESERVE
Facilities: Toilets, showers, car-based campground
Walk-in: 2 mins, 100m, easy

ⓘ A popular, council-run campground, fronting a long, sandy stretch of river. There are spots just deep enough for adults to dip, but the shallow water is ideally suited for children to frolic a week away. Camping fees apply and booking required, see: Hawkesbury.nsw.gov.au

➜ Via end of Hulbert Rd, Upper Colo.
-33.4199, 150.7347 qd

207 COLO RIVER BRIDGE
Walk-in: 1 min, 50m, easy

ⓘ The Colo River here is deep and wide. With graffitied, concrete pylons and the hum of cars passing overhead, it's not pretty – but if you're heading back to Sydney it's a super-convenient place to wash that mountain dirt away.

➜ Via car park on S side of Colo River Bridge, Putty Rd, Colo.
-33.4324, 150.8285

208 GROSE RIVER AT NAVUA RESERVE
Facilities: Toilets, picnic tables, BBQs
Walk-in: 2 mins, 75m, easy

ⓘ Edged by the biggest sandy beach west of Narrabeen, this reserve sits at the junction of the Grose and Nepean Rivers. On sticky evenings the river is full of chattering children and adults, sitting neck-deep in the water – although towards the confluence there are deeper pools for swimming. Horses and dogs are allowed in the reserve, and many owners take a dip with their four-leggeds.

➜ Via end of Grose River Rd, Grose Wold.
-33.6090, 150.6969 ☙

209 SHAWS CREEK POOL
Navigation: Moderate
Descent: 130m
Walk-in: 35 mins, 1km, moderate

ⓘ Small cascades spill into this medium-sized, near-circular waterhole, with long, slumbering tree trunks and stones scattered far below on its sandy floor. Bush extends right to the water, making it a very pretty, if shady, spot.

➜ From the end of Booker Rd, Hawkesbury Heights, go through the bar gate and continue for 100m. Ignore the false path leading R at the turning area, and continue for another 30m to a fork. Bear R and continue for another 400m to a rock outcrop with views over the valley. A path descends steeply through a double-opening chimney to the R. Continue carefully downhill over a slippery leaf-littered path which leads directly to the pool. ⬚ 200m.
-33.6531, 150.6414

210 VICTORIA FALLS
Navigation: Easy
Descent: 360m
Walk-in: 60 mins, 2.2km, moderate

ⓘ Beneath tall, drizzling falls, a small, waist-deep pool of chilly water is dotted with the bright red of freshwater yabbies. You can't really swim here, but it's an impressive place for a plunge.

211 Wollangambe River Canyon Two

Shaw's Creek Pool

➔ From car park at end of unsealed Victoria Falls Rd, Mt Victoria (5km from Hwy), follow signs for Victoria Falls. Path zigzags down, but not overly steeply. First R turn leads to The Cascades – a small waterfall; the second turn-off leads to the top of the falls; while the third leads to the pool at the base.

-33.5731, 150.2979 📖

211 WOLLANGAMBE RIVER CANYON TWO

Facilities: Toilets, wood BBQs, car-based campground at start of walk

Navigation: Hard, Mt Wilson + Wollangambe GR 560619 (entry), GR 571925 (exit)

Descent: 270m

Walk-in: 80 minutes, 2.8km, hard

Walk-out: 80 mins, 2.55km, hard

Lilo: 4–5 hours, 2.3km

ⓘ This is similar to the upriver section of the Wollangambe Canyon, although with more stretches of shallow water and not as many long, deep pools you'll be getting on and off your lilo quite a bit. If, however, you've already explored Wollangambe One and are keen to experience more, then it's worth checking out this less-travelled section of canyon. There's no exit sign, and people have gotten into serious trouble after missing the exit – so don't undertake this trip without any prior canyoning experience. Precautions for Wollangambe One apply.

➔ Via Cathedral Reserve Camping Ground, off Mount Irvine Rd, Mount Wilson. From the bottom of the campground cross road and take the fire trail signed Northern FT that heads L / downhill. The other fire trail on your R will be your exit. After 50m this arrives at a locked gate that says "Private Property" – but respectful access is allowed. The trail undulates around the back of Mt Wilson. After 1.8km turn sharp R onto a path (this is also the exit route of Wollangambe One). This descends a spur, eventually parallel to a small gully, before reaching the river. Near the river there are a couple of tricky climb-downs. At the river there's space to blow up your lilo and get into your wetsuit. Near the start there's an awkward, forced 2m jump into water. A little further on is a deep pool with a good 4m cliff jump option. Travelling downriver, Whungee Whingee Canyon comes in on the L at an angle, just before a massive boulder that blocks most of the river. After WW the canyon becomes more dramatic with high-sided cliffs. Towards the end there's a big block-up with large boulders. Shortly after look out for Waterfall of Moss Canyon coming in on the L. The exit is just a few hundred metres further – this is perhaps the most spectacular section. The exit is on the R-hand side. Watch out for small, sandy landings on either side below steep, rocky gullies. There's no exit sign. However, you should recognise it, as there has been nowhere like it previously. There's a high rock ledge beside the exit on which to get out of your wetsuit. The path climbs very steeply for a few hundred metres, becoming more moderate as you ascend a spur, before reaching an outcrop with fine views. After 1.8km you reach an old fire trail turning circle, before arriving at a T-junction after 2.05km. Turn R. After 2.35km bear L at fork through old gate. It's just another 150m back to the campground.

-33.4868, 150.3746 🅿️🏕️🅿️🥾

Central Coast & Newcastle

Change down a few gears and explore this sprawling coastline and the region's sheltered inland waters. Here it's easy to take it easy!

Highlights
Central Coast &
Newcastle

Our favourites include:

214 Emerald Pool – Take a dip in this remote waterhole, metres from Aboriginal axe-grinding grooves.

215 Maitland Bay – Find the city's beaches too crowded? Head to this wild beach and bathe in its cobalt water in solitude.

217 Merewether Ocean Baths – Get a feel for the real Newcastle by swimming at this local institution.

Freemar

Crumps Retreat

Martinsville

Cooranbo

Mandalong

Lemon Tree

Cedar Brush Creek   Ravensdale   Dooralong

Kiar

Yarramalong   Halloran

Kulnura   Sparks Rd

Wyong Creek   Warnervale

Alison   Wadalt

Mardi

Central Mangrove   Tac

Tuggerah

Upper Mangrove   Palm Grove

Ten Mile Hollow   Palmdale   Kangy Angy

Peats Ridge   Chitta

Mangrove Creek   Glenning Valley

Somersby   Tumbi U

Greengrove   Lisarow

Narara

Laughtondale   Wyoming

Lower Mangrove   **214**   West Gosford   Matcham

Calga   Springfield   Spoon Bay E

Kariong   Erina   Wamber

Gunderman   Tascott   **229**

Marlow   Mooney Mooney Creek   Kincumber

Spencer   **221**   **228**

Singletons Mill   **213**   **220**   **222**   Bensville   **227**

Wondabyne   Woy Woy Bay   Blackwall   **226**

Canoelands   Umina Beach   Bouddi

28   Bar Point   Cogra Bay   **223**   **215**

Coba Point   **224**   **225**

Forest Glen   **Brooklyn** 59   Dangar Island   **219**

Ants Nest Pt   **212**   Box Head

Barnsley

Wakefield

Boolaroo

Kotara

Charlestown

Kahibah

Bar Beach

248
247
218

217

terhole

Ryhope

Fassifern

Booragul

Windale

Dudley

Awaba

Eleebana

244

245

Redhead

243

Valentine

Jewells

241

240 242

246

Buttaba

239

Marks Point

Wangi Road

Dora Creek

Swansea

Windermere Park

238

237

Cams Wharf

236

235 Crangan Bay

Wyee

Mannering Park

Catherine Hill Bay

Doyalson North

Wybung 216

234

San Remo

Budgewoi Peninsula

rah

Lake Haven

Budgewoi

Kanwal

Main Road

Toukley

233

Magenta

y Bay

232

231

230

orresters Beach

ch

Toronto Road

Macquarie Road

Pacific Motorway

The coast between Patonga and Newcastle stretches for more than 90km, but unless you like swimming between the flags, its waters are generally better suited to surfers. If, however, you know where to look, there are some fantastic sheltered beaches and bays that have every bit of the laid-back charm that first popularised the area with sea-changers. This region is in close reach of Sydney, making it perfect for a day-trip or weekend getaway.

Patonga Beach has an unpretentious charm, and feels lazy in the best possible way. It's never had the glamour of neighbouring Pearl Beach, and still remains a fishing village at heart. The houses are mostly small, original, weatherboard and fibro shacks and, although the village is busy during holidays and the pub is lively of a weekend, Patonga retains a nice end-of-the-road tranquility.

The 1.3km, southeast-facing beach is framed by national park and looks across to Barrenjoey Head and Ku-ring-gai. Nestled inside Broken Bay, it's rare for the beach to receive swell, and it has some of the most protected water on the Central Coast. The calmest water is near the ferry wharf, although it's not particularly good for swimming as there's also a boat ramp and moorings. Instead, head to the southern end, backed by a council-run campground.

Kariong Brook Pool. Set in a lush rock ampitheatre, with a 10m-high waterfall, this is a freshwater haven in an overwhelmingly coastal area. It's the perfect antidote for a hot day, as the surrounding trees and rock ledges create a delightfully shady spot.

The light here is beautiful, and when the sun breaks through the tree canopy it bounces off the surface of the water and reflects back on everything in shimmery golden waves. The pool is small, with deep, clear, jade water that's on the chilly side even in summer. Blue-bummed dragonflies streak atop the surface, and the trilling cicadas compete with the din of the high, tumbling waterfall. The thick trunk of an old, fallen tree sits at the end of the pool in a column of sunshine, and is a great spot to dry off.

Emerald Pool. A delightful oasis of tranquil coolness in the harsh Australian bush – you could never guess of its existence, as it appears out of nowhere. It's a lovely place to while away a summer's day.

213 Kariong Brook Pool

212 Patonga Beach

▶

Emerald Pool

212 PATONGA BEACH

Facilities: Toilets, playground in car-based campground

Seclusion: Busy-average

Walk-in: 2 mins, 100m, easy

ⓘ The squeaky sand gently slopes into the gum-coloured water, and it's a good spot for paddlers and swimmers alike. Care needs to be taken if swimming around the creek mouth, though, as there are sometimes strong currents. As you'd expect of a fishing village, Patonga has lots of resident pelicans. These make interesting swimming companions, but they move with surprising ease and grace through the water, so keeping up with them is next to impossible! Camping fees apply and booking required – see Gosford.nsw. gov.au

➔ From car park at S end of Bay St, Patonga, walk through campground gate. Access to the beach is behind playground. 🚆 Patonga Wharf 800m.

-33.5544, 151.2696 🅰 🗺 🚏

213 KARIONG BROOK POOL

Seclusion: Average

Navigation: Easy

Descent: 170m

Walk-in: 50 mins, 2.45km, easy-moderate

➔ From Staples Lookout, Woy Woy Rd, Woy Woy Bay, continue S for 350m and park in small lay-by on opposite side of the road, at start of fire trail. Take gated fire trail signed Brisbane Waters National Park, Thommo's Loop Fire Trail to Great North Walk. Proceed straight across intersection after 170m and continue along this fairly flat trail. After 1.8km turn R onto a track signed Girrakool. This descends sometimes steeply with steps to the pool.

-33.4745, 151.2695 🅱

214 EMERALD POOL

Seclusion: Average

Navigation: Easy-moderate

Descent: 150m

Walk-in: 65 mins, 3.55km, easy-moderate

ⓘ The pool is only about 15m, and though small, it's incredibly beautiful.

The water really is a remarkable emerald green, and when the sun hits its surface, the colour is startling! The sandy bottom and brown yabbies that march, scanning the pool with their little nippers, can all be seen in perfect detail, as though you're looking through glass. The track is exposed with little shade

➔ Via car park at end of Ironbark Rd, Mangrove Mountain. The last 3.5km are unsealed and there's a rough, steep section 850m from the end, which may be unsuitable for 2WD vehicles. From the car park go through the locked gate and walk down the Mt Olive Trail. At the fork after 300m turn L, ignoring the path on the left to Mt Olive after a further 20m. The fire trail descends gently with a few steeper sections. After 2.6km turn R onto Hominy Creek Trail. After 3.45km you arrive at Hominy Creek. Cross over and walk L, downstream a short distance to the pool.

-33.4028, 151.1718

214 Emerald Pool

Hominy Creek pitter-patters into the pool, and the gentle sound is reminiscent of someone running a bath. The creek's catchment is entirely within Popran National Park, so the water's pristine. The pool has a delightful feeling of being tucked away, thanks to the surrounding rock ledges with their banksias and blackboys.

Emerald has a tangible Aboriginal history, as just down the creek bed there are a number of axe-grinding grooves and animal etchings. You can place your hands in the grooves and trace the movement of their makers. It's quite something to swim somewhere that's been used for thousands of years! Please tread lightly and look after this special place, so it can continue to be enjoyed for generations to come!

Maitland Bay. Wild beaches tend to be rough and windswept; this south-facing beach, however, retains a lovely sense of wildness, while still having relatively calm and protected water. There's little trace of humans here, so it's a great place to get away from it all.

Yes, you may have to share it with a few others, but the beach is so large you could easily have hundreds of metres of cobalt water and beautiful, bush-backed sand to yourself. That's equivalent to being the only person in the QVB, or rattling around the SCG by yourself! Where is everybody! No tooting taxis, just the gentle crashing of waves. No asphalt, just squeaking, soft sand. No towering offices, just the sun in the sky. No hurried elbows bumping into you, just salt water drying on your skin.

▶

215 Maitland Bay

Bongon Beach. "Aaaah" is the only sound you're likely to hear, besides the twittering of birds in the surrounding scrubland and the purr of waves breaking at nearby Frazers Beach. The "aaaah" will rise up from within you, and with it all the stress of the week and the city will fade away. This is a magical spot, combining a beautiful, natural setting with a tranquillity that's sometimes difficult to find in other Central Coast beaches.

Enclosed by Munmorah State Conservation Area, the southwest-facing beach is set inside a small, narrow cove that sits within the greater bay of the more frequented and surf-swept Frazers Beach. It has a feeling of wild seclusion, which is enhanced by being out of sight from the car park above.

Merewether Ocean Baths. These baths are massive – in fact they're the largest ocean baths in the southern hemisphere! Cut out of the intertidal shelf, the whole ocean seems to be before you as you swim. If you make it for an early-morning dip, you might even see dolphins playing in the surf just beyond the pool!

Despite their size, the baths have no delusions of grandeur, and remain charming and refreshingly utilitarian. They're a much-loved Newcastle institution, and the legions of regulars who pound out their daily laps can be found here no matter the weather. Even if you're not an avid lap-swimmer, it's a great place to join in and experience a central part of Novocastrian life.

Newcastle Bogey Hole is the oldest rock pool in NSW. It's the quintessential wild swimming spot, slightly rough around the edges and untamed. Unlike at nearby Merewether Baths, visitors don't come here to exercise. Instead, they come to potter around the pool – to watch fish hide in crevices, to touch delicate grasses clinging to roughly hewn walls and to hear the roar of the ocean beyond.

As you luxuriate in the Bogey Hole, spare a thought for its makers: in 1819 Commandant Morrisset forced some convicts to create the pool solely for his own use!

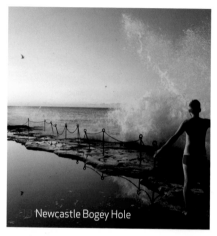

Newcastle Bogey Hole

218 Newcastle Bogey Hole

217 Merewether Ocean Baths

215 MAITLAND BAY

Seclusion: Average-secluded
Navigation: Easy
Descent: 150m
Walk-in: 20 mins, 900m, easy-moderate
ⓘ The far end of the beach is the most protected and best for swimming. The water drops off suddenly, but the waves are usually gentle and low.

→ From car park at junction of Maitland Bay Dr and The Scenic Rd, Killcare Heights, take track to L of entrance. This descends gently to the beach. ☐ 0m.

-33.5231, 151.3913 ▣

216 BONGON BEACH

Facilities: Campground at Frazers Beach, 350m around the headland
Seclusion: Average-secluded
Navigation: Easy
Descent: 20m
Walk-in: 5 mins, 140m, moderate
ⓘ Despite being only narrowly separated from the weather-beaten coastline, it receives only small, refracted waves. The striking

aquamarine water never gets overly deep and has good visibility. It's remarkably little visited, with fishermen a more common sight than swimmers. Camping fees apply and booking required – contact NPWS.

→ Travelling N on the Pacific Hwy, turn R onto Blue Wren Dr, Wybung, to enter Munmorah State Recreation Area (vehicle entry fees apply). After 1.6km turn L onto Campbell Dr. After 5.5km this becomes unsealed Snapper Point Rd. After 6.7km arrive at car park. Follow narrow path leading from the bottom R corner of the car park.

-33.1864, 151.6265 ▣ ▲

217 MEREWETHER OCEAN BATHS

Facilities: Toilets, change-rooms, picnic tables
Seclusion: Busy
Walk-in: 1 min, 25m, easy
ⓘ The baths are divided roughly in two, with a mixed-use lap pool and sandy-beached paddling pool. The main pool, at 100 x 50m, is so enormous that, unusually, laps are swum across

its width, rather than length. Iconic-numbered starting blocks, which appear to be cut from a sandcastle, stand at either end of the lap area. Baths are closed for cleaning, see: Newcastle.nsw.gov.au

→ Via Henderson Pde, Mereweather. ☐ 250m.

-32.9517, 151.7556 ▣ ▣

218 NEWCASTLE BOGEY HOLE

Seclusion: Busy-average
Walk-in: 5 mins, 250m, easy-moderate
ⓘ Hidden beneath steep-sided cliffs that drop away into the ocean, the Bogey Hole is cut out of the rock shelf and is irregularly shaped, with no straight lines. The 25m pool is rustic and real, and waves crash into the outer-lying rocks, sending white frothy droplets hailing into it. Inside, the water remains calm, and orange starfish cling to pebbles downy with green fuzz.

→ Take steps down from York Dr, Newcastle, or walk to southern end of Shortland Esplanade. ☐ 500m.

213 Kariong Brook Pool

And if you have time...

219 PEARL BEACH & ROCK POOL

Facilities: Toilets, playground
Walk-in: 5 mins, 200m, easy

ⓘ This southeast-facing beach overlooks Broken Bay, and is an ever-popular holiday destination for Sydney-siders. As houses line its length it's not particularly inspiring, but the southern end has calm water, good for swimming, as well as a 30m, pumped rock pool.

→ Via car park at S end of Pearl Pde, Pearl Beach. 🚗 0m.

-33.5453,151.3081 🛟

220 WOY WOY BATHS

Facilities: Toilets, playground
Walk-in: 1 min, 10m, easy

ⓘ This is the best tidal bath within Brisbane Water, and despite being next to a rather busy suburban road, the outlook is quite green. The baths are 40m long and enclosed by a boardwalk. As the water reaches 2.8m, swimming is possible even at low tide, which is somewhat of a rarity in the area. The baths are next to a popular fish and chip shop, with its seemingly ever-present pelicans.

→ Via Brick Wharf Rd, Woy Woy, nr junction with The Boulevard. 🚆 Woy Woy Station 350m.

-33.4837,151.3263 🛟 🍴

221 YATTALUNGA BATHS

Walk-in: 2 mins, 100m, easy

ⓘ This bath is unique in that it doesn't front the shoreline; instead you must walk 100m along a boardwalk just to reach the small enclosure. This means you bypass the estuarine shallows of Brisbane Water, and, at least at high tide, you can punch out some laps. The residential location ensures it's a quiet spot.

→ Via S end of Mundoora Ave, Yattalunga. 🚗 200m.

-33.4687, 151.3590

222 DAVISTOWN BATHS

Facilities: Toilets, picnic tables, playground
Walk-in: 1 min, 30m, easy

ⓘ This shallow, 40m tidal bath with a grassy reserve on Brisbane Water, is popular with families, despite being adjacent to a busy boating thoroughfare.

→ Via S end of Pine Ave, Davistown. 🚢 Davistown Pine Av Wharf 70m.

-33.4902,151.3639 🛟

223 PRETTY BEACH BATHS

Facilities: Toilets, change-rooms
Walk-in: 1 min, 5m, easy

These baths have a roadside location just inside the entrance of Brisbane Water. The netted 50m enclosure has suffered from siltation, and for adults a high tide swim is best.

→ Via E end of Pretty Beach Rd, Pretty Beach. 🚗 5m.

-33.5260,151.3493

225 Putty Beach

224 Lobster Beach

224 LOBSTER BEACH
Navigation: Easy
Descent: 50m
Walk-in: 10 mins, 300m, moderate
ⓘ This 300m, west-facing beach has a pretty national park setting, and makes an easy, bush escape. However, its calm water within Broken Bay is a popular place to drop anchor, which can detract from the tranquility.

→ Via path off Highview Rd nr junction with Venice Rd, Pretty Beach. Path ascends before descending to beach. 🔲 300m.
-33.5296,151.3411 🖼

225 PUTTY BEACH
Facilities: Toilets, showers, picnic tables, BBQs, campground
Walk-in: 1 min, 50m, easy
ⓘ As the northern half of surfy Killcare Beach, Putty offers much better conditions for swimming. The southwest-facing beach is backed by national park; the surroundings are also more natural. It's a very popular

spot, and as you can drive right to it, it's a great choice for families. There's also a campsite just 50m from the beach. Camping fees apply and booking required – contact NPWS.

→ Via car park at end of Putty Beach Dr, Killcare. Vehicle entry fees apply.
-33.5292,151.3741 🔺 🖼

226 MACMASTERS BEACH ROCK POOL
Facilities: Toilets, kiosk
Walk-in: 1 min, 50m, easy
ⓘ A shallow children's pool.

→ Via S end of Marine Pde, MacMasters Beach. 🔲 900m.
-33.5009,151.4258 🏊 🍴

227 COPACABANA BOGEY HOLE
Walk-in: 2 min, 70m, easy
ⓘ A pretty decent, large bogey hole that's probably at its best mid to low tide.

→ Via path at junction of Del Monte Pl and Del Rio Dr, Copacabana. 🔲 400m.
-33.4912,151.4346 🏊

228 AVOCA BEACH BOGEY HOLE
Facilities: Toilets, showers, kiosk
Walk-in: 5 mins, 200m, easy
ⓘ A shallow bogey hole for paddlers.

→ Via end of Avoca Dr, Avoca, nr junction with Cliff Ave. 🔲 150m.
-33.4701,151.4374 🏊 🍴

229 TERRIGAL HAVEN
Facilities: Toilets, change-rooms, showers, picnic tables, BBQs, kiosk
Walk-in: 1 min, 40m, easy
ⓘ A northwest-facing beach with a large expanse of flat, calm ocean, and a number of buoys placed at intervals offshore to mark swimming routes.

→ Via car park off S end of Terrigal Esp, Terrigal. 🔲 600m.
-33.4479,151.4486 🏖

Lake Munmorah Swim Enclosure

230 BATEAU BAY

Facilities: Toilets, picnic tables
Descent: 20m
Walk-in: 5 mins, 150m, easy-moderate
(i) Much of the coastline between Terrigal and The Entrance is fringed by large houses and cafés, but this 200m, south-facing beach is enclosed by the last patch of coastal rainforest left in the area. The northeastern end is the best for swimming.

→ Via path descending from car park on Reserve Dr, Bateau Bay, nr junction with Harbour St. 🚗 300m.

-33.3828,151.4857 🏖

231 TOOWOON BAY

Facilities: Toilets, picnic tables, kiosk
Walk-in: 1 min, 50m, easy
(i) A suburban spot, popular with families. The southern end of this northeast-facing beach is the most protected, and best for swimming.

→ Via car park off S end of Bay Rd, Toowoon Bay. 🚗 150m.

-33.3618,151.5010 🍴 🏖

232 THE ENTRANCE OCEAN BATHS

Walk-in: 1 min, 50m, easy
(i) Formerly a simple rock pool, today the YMCA manage this pumped, multi-pool complex – the only ocean baths on the Central Coast. Open 8:30am – 5:00pm.

→ Via car park at end of Boondilla Rd, The Entrance. 🚗 650m.

-33.3502,151.5035

233 NORAH HEAD BOGEY HOLE

Facilities: Toilets, showers
Walk-in: 1 min, 60m, easy
(i) A shallow, 55m ring of rocks, good for paddlers.

→ Via car park at end of Bald St, Norah Head. 🚗 300m.

-33.2789,151.5695 🏖

234 LAKE MUNMORAH SWIM ENCLOSURE

Facilities: Toilet, picnic tables, BBQs
Walk-in: 1 min, 30m, easy
This massive coastal lagoon never reaches a depth greater than 2m. The shark-free water is usually perfectly flat. If you fancy swimming outside the net, keep a lookout for boats – you might have to do that anyway as the 60m enclosure is shallow and pretty weedy.

→ Via end of Dianne Ave, Munmorah. 🚗 200m.

-33.1961,151.5755 🏄

235 GWANDALAN BATHS

Facilities: Toilets, picnic tables, BBQs, playground
Walk-in: 1 min, 5m, easy
(i) A 32m enclosure with jetty that suffers from litter.

→ Via end of Koowong Rd, Gwandalen. 🚗 210m.

-33.1382,151.5877

236 SUMMERLAND POINT SWIM ENCLOSURE

Facilities: Toilets, picnic tables, BBQs, playground

Walk-in: 1 min, 30m, easy

ⓘ This 60m, netted enclosure is by far the nicest in the area. Set within a bushy reserve, the waist-deep water and the sandy bottom is weed-free!

→ Via Sandy Beach Reserve at W end of Kullaroo Rd, Summerland Point. 650m.

-33.1385, 151.5565

237 BRIGHTWATERS BATHS

Facilities: Toilets, picnic tables

Walk-in: 1 min, 10m, easy

ⓘ This narrow, 25m enclosure has a jetty and suitably deep water with good clarity. A power station can be seen across the lake, but this is still one of the nicest enclosures in the area.

→ Via end of Lake View Ave, Brightwaters. 250m.

-33.1184, 151.5458

238 SUNSHINE BATHS

Facilities: Toilets

Walk-in: 2 mins, 100m, easy

ⓘ The lovely painted sign at the top of the park is the best thing about this 30m, suburban bath.

→ Via Sunshine Pde, Sunshine, nr junction with Cessnock Rd. 0m.

-33.1127,151.5661

239 ACADIA VALE BATHS

Facilities: Toilets, shower, picnic tables, BBQs, playground

Walk-in: 1 min, 20m, easy

ⓘ A 45m enclosure and jetty, backed by a quiet suburban park.

→ Via end of Brooks St, Arcadia Vale. 80m.

-33.0620,151.5874

240 RATHMINES BATHS

Walk-in: 1 min, 20m, easy

ⓘ A small enclosure surrounded by parks and playing fields.

→ Via N end of Stilling St, Rathmines. 700m.

-33.0392, 151.5982

241 KILABEN BAY BATHS

Facilities: Toilets, picnic tables, BBQs, playground

Walk-in: Easy. 50m one way

ⓘ A 60m enclosure with a jetty and deep water, between residential blocks.

→ Via Kilaben Rd, Kilaben Bay, nr junction with Jarrett St. 100m.

-33.0268, 151.5930

242 COAL POINT BATHS

Walk-in: 1 min, 20m, easy

ⓘ A narrow, 30m enclosure with a wooden jetty.

→ Via E end of Rofe St, Coal Point. 210m.

-33.0407, 151.6148

237 Brightwaters Baths

247 Newcastle Ocean Baths

243 TORONTO BATHS
Facilities: Toilets, picnic tables, BBQs, kiosk
Walk-in: 1 min, 30m, easy
ⓘ 50m baths with deep water and wrap-around jetty, in a boring urban location.
➜ Via S end of Victory Pde, Toronto. 🅿 5m.
-33.0141, 151.5989 🍴🍴

244 BOLTON BATHS
Facilities: Toilets
Walk-in: 1 min, 15m, easy
ⓘ A 30m enclosure with deep water and a jetty, backed by a suburban park.
➜ Via Prospect Ave, Bolton Point. 🅿 900m.
-32.9983, 151.6092 🍴

245 VALENTINE BATHS
Facilities: Toilets, showers, picnic tables
Walk-in: 1 min, 10m, easy
ⓘ A 60m enclosure in a suburban park, bounded on two sides by a wharf, with deep water for jumping.
➜ Off Valentine Cres, Valentine, nr bowling club. 🅿 620m.
-33.0037, 151.6402 🍴

246 BELMONT BATHS
Facilities: Toilets, picnic tables
Walk-in: 1 min, 25m, easy
ⓘ A 65m enclosure with jetty, that suffers from litter and traffic noise.
➜ Off Brooks Pde, Belmont, nr junction with Maude St. 🅿 20m.
-33.0341, 151.6560

247 NEWCASTLE OCEAN BATHS
Facilities: Toilets, change-rooms
Walk-in: 1 min, 25m, easy
ⓘ A 50m lap pool, 75m free-swimming area, and a 100m kiddie pool, backed by a shabby, art deco bathers' pavilion and

a wide concrete beach. Closed once a week for cleaning. See Newcastle.nsw.gov.au/recreation
➜ Via Shortland Esp, Newcastle East, nr Tramway Reserve. 🚉 Newcastle Station 750m.
-32.9295, 151.7908 🏊

248 SOLDIERS POINT POOL
Facilities: Picnic tables
Walk-in: 1 min, 50m, easy
ⓘ A large, dilapidated bogey hole, that's good for swimming in calm weather.
➜ Via car park at N end of Shortland Esp, Newcastle East. 🚉 Newcastle Station 900m.
-32.9253, 151.7931 🏊

Bateau Bay

Safety

It's common sense stuff, but here's a list of safety tips:

- Be realistic – stay within your limits
- Don't swim under the influence of drugs or alcohol
- Be sun smart – you know the drill: slip, slop and slap!
- Plan ahead – check conditions before leaving home
- Don't swim for at least three days after rain – urban run-off and sewerage overflow affect water quality
- Observe conditions and don't assume that somewhere that was safe in the past is still safe – look for speed of flow in rivers and keep out if in flood.

Jumping safety

- Understand the risks – jumps can result in serious injury
- Check the depth and for any obstructions - you need to get into the water to do this properly
- Jump feet first
- Be decisive – injuries are more likely to occur if you falter as you jump
- Jump well clear of the edge.

Beach safety

The beaches in this book have a Surf Life Saving Australia hazard rating of 4 or less out of 10. Note, however, that these ratings only apply under normal conditions. When there's a swell swimming will be less safe.

The beaches in this book have been chosen for their safe swimming conditions, including a lack of rips. That said, you may still encounter one.

What to do if you get caught in a rip

- Stay calm
- Raise your arm to signal that you're in difficulty
- Don't try to swim directly back to shore, against the rip, instead swim parallel to the beach towards the breaking waves
- Reserve your energy by floating on your back. The rip may flow in a circular pattern and return you to a sandbar where you can exit the water.

Sharks

Shark attacks are exceedingly rare, but here's some precautionary tips:

- Don't swim during the night or at dawn or dusk – prime feeding time for sharks
- Don't swim in murky water – sharks prefer being less visible to their prey
- Avoid swimming near steep drop-offs – favoured feeding grounds.

Stingers

If you are stung by a bluebottle or jellyfish:

- Wash off any remaining tentacles with seawater
- Apply a cold pack, or wrapped ice, for at least 10 minutes, or until pain is relieved
- Seek medical assistance if condition deteriorates.

Bush Safety

There are particular considerations to be aware of in the bush, because help is rarely close to hand:

- Underestimate your abilities – walks tend to take longer than you anticipate
- Don't go on your own – friends can go for help
- Tell someone of your plans – provide thorough details of where you plan to go and when you expect to be back, so they can raise the alarm if you don't return
- Know what you're getting in to and be prepared – read all directions and notes, and check on the latest conditions before you go
- Travel in daylight only – be out of the bush or at camp by dusk, as it's very easy to become disorientated and lost in the darkness
- Protect yourself from the elements – wear suitable clothing and footwear
- Stay hydrated.

If you become lost

- Stay calm, stop and think
- Recheck directions
- Retrace your steps a short distance. Locate your last known point if possible
- Gain some height which may assist in orientation
- If the above does not help stay where you are
- Find shelter, stay warm and dry
- Activate your Personal Locator Beacon (PLB). See Before you go, on how to hire a PLB
- Attempt to make your position visible to searchers from land and air, e.g. light a small fire or place bright clothing in an open area
- If you are in a group stay together
- Be aware it can take a considerable time for rescuers to reach you. Your priority is to remain warm and dry. Ration food and water if necessary.

Campfires

- Observe fire bans
- Use existing fire sites where possible
- Place fires in a cleared space – away from grass, leaves and vegetation

- Don't have a fire or stove in or near your tent
- Put out fires before bed

Snakes

- Make noise – generally snakes are more scared of us, then we are of them
- Keep your eyes peeled – a snake caught unawares can be dangerous
- If you do see a snake – stop and remain still until it clears off. If you unexpectedly stumble upon one, retreat slowly, keeping it in your sight
- Wear sturdy, covered footwear – that can help the severity of a bite.

Snake bite care

- Rest and reassure the patient
- Apply a broad pressure bandage over the bite site as soon as possible: the bandage should be firm and tight. If you don't have an elasticised bandage, use a piece of clothing
- Apply a further pressure bandage: start just above the fingers or toes, and move upwards on the limb as far as can be reached (include the snake bite). Apply tightly without stopping blood supply to the limb
- Splint the bandaged limb
- Ensure the patient does not move
- Write down the time of the bite and when the bandage was applied
- Stay with the patient and send someone for help
- Check circulation in fingers or toes

Wild Swimming
Sydney Australia

250 best rock pools, beaches, rivers and waterholes

Words & Photos:
Sally Tertini
Steve Pollard

Editing:
Lucie Wood

Proofing:
Georgia Laval

Design and Layout:
Oliver Mann
Dermot Rushe

Series Concept:
Daniel Start

UK Distribution:
Central Books Ltd
99 Wallis Road, London, E9 5LN
Tel +44 (0)845 458 9911
orders@centralbooks.com

Published by:
Wild Things Publishing Ltd.
Freshford, Bath, BA2 7WG
BA2 7WG,
United Kingdom
hello@wildthingspublishing.com

We'd love to hear from you!
To give feedback or share a favourite swim spot, visit

www.wildswimming.com.au

hello@wildthingspublishing.com
hello@wildswimming.com

Copyright

Author acknowledgements: With thanks to the Pulsar, Cool Bananas and the Cheerful Cherry for getting us on the road, and never leaving us stuck in the bush; our parents for never saying that we were wasting our time, and for putting up with either sand being traipsed through their house, or with us being in a different country; Jamie and Laura for their ongoing friendship and support; and finally to Daniel Start, for making dreams come true by believing in this project enough to include it in his inspiring Wild Swimming series!

Dedicated to Sally, for this greatest adventure: for always being happy to jump in and explore around the next corner, as well as for bringing out the Bean Fantasy when the the going got tough; and to Rosy for inspiring this journey.

Also to the wild ones of past, present and future: Grandma, who sadly never learnt to swim, but who always had a twinkle in her eye; Nonna, who felt truly free, swimming out past the breakers; Nonno, who is still known to dive in, at 92; my parents who took me into the bush, despite my protests, and who let me explore, unhindered, the nooks and crannies of our watery backyard; Steve, the best companion with which to navigate the wild and the mundane. Thank you for making this crazy idea grow into something real, for always striving to keep me wild at heart, and for the cicada; Brilli, who I hope forever remembers to follow the wild yearnings of her heart, and grows up with a deep appreciation of the natural world. May you come to love some of the special places in this book, and too, discover your own wild places of magic. Finally, to Mr Webster, who didn't seem very wild in the shallow end of Ashfield Pool, but who gave me a great gift in teaching me to swim.

Further reading:

Blossom, L. Splash – Great Writing About Swimming. New Jersey: The Ecco Press, 1996

Deakin, R. Waterlog. London: Vintage, 2000

Kellerman, A. How to Swim. New York: George H. Doran, 1918

Sprawson, C. Haunts of the Black Masseur – The Swimmer as Hero. London: Vintage, 1993

Start, D. Wild Swimming - 300 Hidden Dips in the Rivers, Lakes and Waterfalls of UK, 1998

Winton, T. Land's Edge: A Coastal Memoir. London: Picador, 2014